THE NEXT BIG CRASH

CONSPIRACY, COLLAPSE, AND THE MEN
BEHIND HISTORY'S BIGGEST HEIST

WRITTEN BY

JUSTIN HASKINS

CONTRIBUTOR
JACK MCPHERRIN

OUR
REPUBLIC

THE
HEARTLAND
INSTITUTE

The Next Big Crash:
Conspiracy, Collapse, and the Men Behind History's Biggest Heist

Published by Our Republic and The Heartland Institute, Schaumburg, IL.

Distributed by Kindle Direct Publishing.

Paperback Print ISBN: 978-1-970299-02-1

Cover Design by Alexander Somoskey and Donald Kendal.

Interior Design by Donald Kendal.

Printed in the United States of America.

CONTENTS

ACKNOWLEDGMENTS

I would like to thank Bette and Don Grande and Audrea Decker for their tireless efforts to defend freedom across all fifty states, especially on the issues at the heart of this book. Their dedication has been an inspiration to me and to countless others who share in the struggle for liberty.

I am deeply indebted to David Rogers Webb, one of the world's foremost experts on the dangers of concentrated securities ownership. Without his extraordinary investigative work, this book would not have been possible. He deserves far more recognition than he will ever receive for exposing the deeply troubling realities surrounding the Depository Trust Company and the financial system it underpins.

I also wish to thank Glenn Beck, who has taught me the importance of questioning with boldness, even when doing so brings controversy or conflict. His friendship, mentorship, and partnership have been invaluable in my lifelong fight to see America become a freer and more prosperous nation.

Finally, and above all, I thank God for the countless blessings He has poured into my life. I am not worthy of them, yet I remain forever grateful.

1

THE NEXT BIG CRASH

BLACK MONDAY: THE CARTER FAMILY

October 5 – 8:04 a.m. Mountain Time – Millcreek, Utah
(Monday Morning)

The hum of the refrigerator was the only sound in the Carter household, until the sharp chime of Michael's phone vibrating on the nightstand shattered the silence.

He didn't recognize the number, but something about the early hour made him answer.

"Michael, it's Brian from the office. Don't come in today. Actually, don't log in to anything. Just turn on the news."

The line went dead.

Michael sat up straight, confusion still heavy in his groggy brain. Beside him, Emily stirred under the covers. He grabbed the remote and clicked on the TV.

ABC News. The screen was already splattered in red. The anchor's voice held calm, but her eyes showed panic.

"We are continuing to follow breaking news this morning. Both the New York Stock Exchange and Nasdaq have been taken offline following what federal cybersecurity officials are now calling a coordinated AI-powered cyberattack, believed to have originated from a foreign adversary. Trading was halted just minutes after the opening bell, and federal authorities have since suspended all market activity indefinitely."

Michael blinked.

He felt like someone had punched a hole through the floor of his world.

October 5 – 8:26 a.m. Mountain Time – The Slide Begins

The sell-off had begun the moment traders realized what was happening. Despite halts, despite warnings, panic tore through digital trading platforms like wildfire.

Even before the government's emergency freeze on all financial transactions—bank withdrawals, investment accounts, even basic retail trading—trillions had been sucked out of the system.

Digital queues crashed. Algorithms glitched. Clearing and settling platforms became overwhelmed and unresponsive.

By the time Michael checked his brokerage account, it was too late.

"Temporarily unavailable. Please try again later," the screen read.

That phrase would haunt him for weeks.

In the hour between the market open at 7:30 a.m. and Michael pouring the day's first cup of coffee, nearly every major Wall Street institution had lost access to critical market infrastructure. Derivatives, swaps, and leveraged portfolios, some layered dozens of times over, were exposed to free fall.

"This is a liquidity death spiral," a breathless guest said on ABC

News. "Firms are drowning, and they can't unwind anything. Nothing. Every player is frozen."

October 5 – 9:51 a.m. Mountain Time – Federal Intervention

Before noon, the president had spoken.

To prevent an all-out collapse of the U.S. financial system, the federal government—with support from the Treasury, federal regulatory agencies, and the Federal Reserve—used emergency powers laws to freeze all institutional and retail financial transactions for the remainder of the day, including commercial and personal banking activity. No one could buy. No one could sell. No one could withdraw.

Michael stared at the screen, motionless. Not even his savings account was accessible. He and Emily had just sent in their mortgage payment. Their credit cards were maxed out from the family's summer road trip through Bryce Canyon and Zion. Payday was supposed to be Friday.

He looked over at Emily, who stood frozen by the doorway, holding their daughter in her arms.

Theadora—three years old, still in fuzzy unicorn pajamas—blinked up at the flashing images on the screen and whispered, "Papa, what's wrong?"

Michael didn't know how to answer. He gave a tight smile and said nothing.

October 6 to 25 – The Long Panic

The days crawled by. Wall Street was cracking at the edges. Firms whispered to be overleveraged had no buyers and no escape. Credit markets locked. Big banks wouldn't lend to smaller ones without grotesque amounts of collateral—collateral that didn't exist. There was simply too much risk. No institution wanted to take a chance when another cyberattack could be right around the corner.

And for once, the Fed did nothing.

The inflation crisis endured during the Biden administration still loomed in every policymaker's mind. Americans were only just recovering from skyrocketing prices, fueled by the U.S. Federal Reserve's injection of gobs of money into circulation—sums technically countable but hard to imagine in practice.

The Fed's strategy, termed "quantitative easing" (QE), had set an inflationary trap over the past decade. Unchecked federal spending over the same period—including direct payments from the Treasury to Americans during and after the COVID-19 pandemic—had sprung the trap. Prices went stratospheric. So did banking interest rates, the Fed's attempt to staunch the bleeding. Eventually, prices stabilized, but few fell to their starting points. To many, the Fed's cure was worse than its disease.

Now, with markets in spiral, the political fallout from another round of emergency QE was unthinkable. So, the Fed held back.

That's when Congress passed a new—and unprecedented—piece of emergency legislation.

Sixteen days into the freeze, the president signed a sweeping executive order that allowed broker-dealers to use customers' securities as collateral in lending agreements with banks and the Federal Reserve. Put simply, to keep Wall Street afloat, Washington gave brokers the ability to secure loans using their customers' investments.

It was pitched as temporary, technical, and "necessary to restore order."

Michael barely noticed at first. Bank accounts frozen, his employer couldn't make payroll. Michael was furloughed until further notice.

The family had other problems, too. Gas stations in Millcreek were requiring exact change for all purchases, and the Smith's Food and Drug down the street had posted handwritten "cash only" signs. Emily was rationing formula and toddler snacks while Theadora asked if they could still go to the "pancake restaurant" that Saturday.

But then, on Monday, October 26, the markets reopened. And everything imploded.

October 26 – The Collapse

The moment trading opened, everyday Americans like Michael flooded the system with sell orders.

It was the only logical move: Get out while you still can. His brokerage account, his 401(k), his Roth IRA, even the modest college savings account they'd started for Theadora—he attempted to sell it all within minutes of the market opening. Trading slowed dramatically. Orders went unfilled. Broker-dealers simply couldn't keep up.

Then, the flood of redemptions caused something far worse.

Broker-dealers couldn't meet their obligations to financial institutions. Their collateral—many of Michael's investments—had already been pledged in high-risk lending deals. When those firms began to fail, the investments used as collateral were gobbled up by banks desperate to stay afloat.

Michael's account balance plummeted overnight.

October 29 – Ground Zero

Outside, the neighborhood in Millcreek looked the same.

Inside, the world had changed.

The Carter family was broke. Unemployment was spiking. Banks weren't issuing new credit. Crime was rising even in places like Salt

Lake County. Trucks were parked at the edge of cities, unsure if their fuel cards would be honored. Grocery stores closed early. Gas and other essentials became hard to come by. And through it all, the president assured the nation that "stability is returning."

But Michael could see it in Emily's eyes. And in his own reflection. Stability was a memory.

Theadora curled up on the couch beside him, unaware that her college fund no longer existed. She giggled at an old episode of a cartoon saved on their tablet, completely untouched by the storm outside.

Michael wished he could freeze that moment.

Because the floor had given way. And no one—not the brokers, not the Fed, not even the most powerful government on Earth—was going to catch them.

BLACK MONDAY: THE ETHAN RAINES STORY

October 5 – 9:46 a.m. Eastern Time – Lower Manhattan

Ethan Raines hadn't even finished his coffee.

He was twenty-seven, freshly promoted, and already one of the fastest-rising junior traders at Halberd Sachs, a hybrid brokerage and investment firm parked one block from the New York Stock Exchange. The floor buzzed around him. The Fox Business channel was on mute across six television screens. Fingers danced across keyboards like bees in a mechanical hive.

Ethan was still grinning about the closing bonus from Friday. Five digits. Not bad for someone who still owed Princeton north of $180,000.

Then the lights flickered.

Only for a second. Long enough to make him pause. Long enough for the monitors on Desk 4A to reboot. Long enough to trigger a low, collective murmur that crawled across the floor.

One of the senior analysts—Sterling . . . or was it Stanley?—rose from his desk. "Is anyone else seeing this? I'm frozen."

Ethan looked down. His trade console had disconnected. His chat servers were timing out. His Slack feed said, Connecting …

Boom.

The alert flashed red across his monitor with a thunderclap:

All markets halted.
NYSE + Nasdaq under federal lockdown.
Unconfirmed reports of AI-enabled cyberattack originating from abroad.

Ethan's mouth went dry. That couldn't be real. That was the kind of alert you saw in simulations, drills, or movies. Not live from the actual New York Stock Exchange.

Then came the message that made his stomach drop:

Global trading halt: all algorithmic systems disabled. Incoming orders rejected.

Short. Clinical. Final.

Ethan stared at the screen. That was it. No trades. No hedging. No rebalancing. Wall Street's most powerful tools had all gone dark, including automated execution engines, predictive liquidity models, and real-time hedging. It didn't matter how smart you were or how much capital you had lined up. There was no one on the other side of the trade.

"What does that even mean?" someone asked from two terminals over, voice tight.

"It means we're sitting on a powder keg," a trader muttered, "and the fuse is already lit."

October 5 – 10:33 a.m. Eastern Time – The Panic Room

Within minutes, the managing partners had locked down the boardroom. Ethan wasn't senior enough to be inside, but he heard the shouting through the reinforced glass.

By 10:02 a.m., the government had frozen all institutional and retail financial activity, everything from money market redemptions to wire transfers. Even internal treasury notes were unresponsive. The entire derivatives division of Halberd Sachs, valued in the billions, was now a black hole in the company's digital ledger.

"Liquidity's gone," someone said near the risk desk.

"Gone?" Ethan repeated.

He blinked.

He had no idea what to say. In school, you studied worst-case scenarios like puzzles. Now he was standing in the middle of one.

October 6 to 25 – War Rooms and Silence

Over the following days, Halberd Sachs became a bunker.

The firm cleared out two conference rooms and turned them into triage centers. Every screen showed the same thing: collateral calls, counterparty risk charts, the real-time heartbeat of a dying financial organism.

But no one could act. No one could trade.

Ethan sat in meeting after meeting while managing directors argued about repo exposure, synthetic shortfalls, and whether it was legal to use retail client portfolios as collateral in a time of crisis.

Then came the news. Congress had passed an act allowing the

THE NEXT BIG CRASH   15

emergency liquidation of assets, and the president had signed it into law. It was followed immediately by an executive order authorizing the use of customer securities as institutional collateral.

The silence in the room was so sharp it felt surgical.

Ethan didn't speak. But he watched. Men in thousand-dollar suits began calculating how to repackage customer portfolios and push them into overnight lending channels. They talked in probabilities. They used acronyms. They never used words like *stealing*.

And Ethan? He nodded, too.

He didn't want to be the one who got iced out of the next bonus round. He didn't want to ask if they were really going to dip into people's IRAs, their retirement, their kids' college funds. He didn't want to be the junior analyst in a suit three years too small for his ambition.

So, he nodded. And when they needed someone to help pull together clients' portfolios to secure an important lending agreement, he did it.

October 26 – The Trigger

When markets reopened, Halberd Sachs braced for a tsunami of redemptions. And that's exactly what came.

Everyday investors, millions of them, fled the equity markets in panic. Ethan watched dashboards blaze red as both individuals and institutions dumped positions, hollowed out portfolios, and triggered a chain reaction in the derivatives market. Then the real collapse began.

One by one, brokers toppled under the weight of their liabilities. Customer accounts, pledged as collateral, evaporated with them. Ethan sat frozen as billions of dollars vanished from the system in less than an hour.

A managing director turned to him and muttered, "This is worse than '08. This is scorched earth."

Ethan said nothing. He stared at the screen as a torrent of notices scrolled past—thousands of nameless accounts in his portfolio were flagged for having "unavailable assets." Then, amid the blur, a single entry froze him:

Michael Carter – 401(k), equity portfolio – "Assets unavailable."
Location: Millcreek, Utah

Just another client on a spreadsheet. A guy in Utah. Probably had a wife. A kid. Maybe a house in a subdivision.

Ethan lingered on the name. Then he closed the tab. What else could he do?

November 3 – The Switch

Ethan sat alone at his desk. The office was nearly silent. Halberd Sachs had lost over 40 percent of its client base. Trading volume was a fraction of what it had been just weeks earlier. Everyone knew more layoffs were coming.

He scrolled through the Fed's press release again, reading the headline for the fifth time:

Federal Reserve and Treasury Announce Official Launch of U.S. Digital Dollar Platform

All stimulus, entitlement payments, and regulated consumer transactions to be routed through new FedLedger app

In response to the continuing financial paralysis, Congress has passed the Emergency Digital Stabilization Act, signed late last night by the president, authorizing the full deployment of a central bank digital currency. The launch is also supported by Executive Order 14803, directing federal agencies to transition all public payment systems to the FedLedger architecture.

They were calling it FedCoin on the floor now. Half joking. Half afraid.

Ethan had no idea what would come next. Nobody did. But he knew one thing: This wasn't something that should happen in a country that claims to protect property rights.

THE NEXT BIG CRASH IS CLOSER THAN YOU THINK

What you've just read is fiction. But it's not fantasy.

None of the events in the stories of Michael Carter or Ethan Raines is impossible. In fact, many experts have been preparing for a similar Armageddon scenario for years: a targeted cyberattack on U.S. markets; an overnight freeze in trading; chains of derivatives so complex and interconnected that they collapse like dominos; politicians using emergency powers to suspend the free market and then empowering Wall Street firms to repurpose your assets to back someone else's risk. Existing laws, investigative reports, and economic data suggest that all these things, and other horrible scenarios, could someday occur, perhaps soon.

This book is not about predicting the exact trigger of the next economic crash or guessing when the next crash will happen. It's about helping you understand how quickly, brutally, and irrevocably our system could fall apart when that moment arrives, and what you can do to be prepared—because a crash *is* coming. It is just a matter of *when*. Although it is impossible to know exactly how bad the next crash will be, there are good reasons to believe it could be one of the most disastrous in our history.

While you've been busy living your life—working, taking your kids to baseball games, paying bills, fixing homes, mowing the lawn, trying to pay down student loan debt—some of the most elite and well-financed institutions in the world have been designing the future in the wake of a coming economic catastrophe. They and others have been preparing—in some ways that are good and helpful for all Americans. Other systems and legal changes, however, have been put into place to increase the power of the ruling class.

My goal in this book is to outline two of the most important threats to your freedom that could emerge when the next big crash occurs. I will also identify who the major players are behind these changes and then share what I am doing to prepare for what's coming. Some of what you read will sound, for lack of a better word, *crazy*.

For example, I will explain how a single, little-known institution has managed to become the registered owner of tens of trillions of dollars' worth of Americans' wealth. The majority of Americans don't realize that individuals no longer directly own most of the securities they purchase. Changes made to the Uniform Commercial Code and the rise of centralized depositories and clearing systems have quietly stripped away the individual's legal ownership of stocks and bonds. Instead, a single financial institution called the Depository Trust Company (DTC) is effectively the direct owner of nearly all publicly traded stocks and bonds, which means that investors have only a contractual claim, not true ownership. DTC is a subsidiary of a larger corporation owned by many of the world's largest financial companies. Most individuals and businesses have, without realizing it, lost direct, registered ownership of the investments they have made.

In a major financial crisis, not having direct ownership of securities like stocks and bonds could become more than a legal technicality. It could determine whether you get to keep your investments—or whether they are seized, frozen, or repurposed without your consent.

I will also explain how central banks around the world are developing programmable currencies that could be used to monitor and restrict your personal spending. Some locations have already implemented these tools for economic and social control, while in other locations, such as the United States, many policymakers are waiting for an opportune time—like a large financial crisis—to impose them.

Most disturbing to me are the influential financial institutions and influential figures, including individuals connected to the CIA, who have laid the groundwork for many of these systems over several decades.

I have provided hundreds of citations to verify my research. Do your own homework, and check what I've written. I'm confident that if you do, you will find my assertions to be true.

THE CRASH IS COMING

In the present U.S. economy, many of America's most important economic institutions and markets are in a precarious situation. For decades, business leaders, Wall Street titans, financial institutions, central bankers, and politicians in both political parties have created the conditions for an economic crash, while creating regulations that will protect larger institutions in the next crisis. Regardless of whether the current president can improve the economy in the short term, there are serious, foundational problems that are not being addressed. Those problems will almost certainly result in an economic recession in the short to medium term. America's economy is sick. It might not be exhibiting all the symptoms of an ailing economy just yet, but there are undeniable signals pointing in the direction of disaster.

In the remaining sections of this chapter, I discuss some of the most concerning aspects of the U.S. economy and then lay out a series of potential triggers that could spark a large economic crisis. At the time the final draft of this book was completed, there were many reasons to believe that the economy could be moving in the right direction; however, the fundamental problems outlined below remain.

It may be difficult for many to accept, but America's economy is in grave danger. Most people have no idea how bad things have become. The same was true in the years prior to the Great Depression of the late 1920s and 1930s, as well as in the years before the Great Recession of 2007 to 2009. There are countless other examples from world history as well. Americans generally do not think a catastrophic economic crash is going to happen—but that's precisely what allows for a *crash* to occur, rather than simply a *slow economic decline*. Economic panic occurs most often because people don't expect something horrible to happen, even when the signs are there for anyone to see. In market-based economies, crashes are inevitable, so it is important to understand the risks so you can guard yourself against the worst of the impacts.

I do hope I am wrong. I hope that our current prosperity only grows—and grows in a linear fashion, with no major economic setbacks. But I do not believe that that is likely, as you will see in the rest of this chapter. Regardless of what occurs, though, one thing is certain: the current situation is dire.

THE NATIONAL DEBT CRISIS

No market-based economy, no matter how large, is immune to downturns. But what's currently brewing is a crisis much larger than a minor recession. Our economy is built on a fragile web of institutions that recklessly gamble on Wall Street; an irresponsible federal government that continues to rack up trillions in debt; and a central bank, the Federal Reserve, that has pumped an unprecedented amount of money into our economy in recent years, making it look as if our country is financially healthier than it really is. America's institutions appear to have built a house of cards, and when it collapses, it's going to be very ugly.

Much of the U.S. economy is built on debt, not economic growth. This has been true for the better part of the past half century, but the debt is now approaching an unsustainable level.

In 1945, the U.S. national debt reached approximately $259 billion, due largely to the costs of World War II—a dramatic increase from about $43 billion in 1940. At the time, this was an unprecedented sum. Over the next few decades, the debt continued to grow, reaching $458 billion by 1973. That same year, President Richard Nixon formally ended the Bretton Woods system, severing the U.S. dollar's convertibility into gold, a process that had begun with his suspension of gold convertibility in 1971. This action effectively transformed the U.S. dollar into a fiat currency, meaning its value was no longer tied to a tangible asset like gold but instead backed solely by government decree. Without the constraints of a gold standard, the federal government gained greater flexibility to expand the money supply, fueling a long-term increase in government spending and national debt.[1,2]

Just one decade after Nixon ended the gold standard, the national debt hit $1.37 trillion. A decade later, in 1993, the debt was $4.41 trillion. That means the national debt had increased by 860 percent in just twenty years.[3] The problem grew even larger in the decades that followed.

From 1993 to the end of President George W. Bush's term in office (January 2009), the national debt increased from $4.41 trillion to $11.91 trillion. During President Barack Obama's two terms, the national debt increased by another $9.32 trillion, reaching a total of $19.95 trillion. By the time Obama left office, the debt had soared to nearly $20 trillion. President Donald Trump did even worse in his first term, adding $7.8 trillion in new debt in just four years, with much of the debt coming in his final ten months in office, due to the COVID-19 pandemic leading to government lockdowns and the implementation of relief programs.[4]

President Joe Biden poured more gasoline on the fire. The federal government added $6.52 trillion in debt during Biden's one term, the highest amount recorded in U.S. history for a president, if you exclude Trump's one COVID-19 year.[5]

At the time I am writing this chapter, halfway through 2025, the current national debt has reached $37 trillion. That means the national debt has tripled since 2009 and increased more during the Obama, Trump, and Biden administrations than it did during every other U.S. presidency in history *combined*.[6] It should go without saying, but I will say it anyway: these figures make it apparent that government spending has become completely out of control.

In the United States' first 150 years, the federal government added $20.6 billion in debt. In the century since, it has added $37 trillion. That means the U.S. government now adds more debt *every four days* than it added in the first 150 years.

The federal government's reckless spending has created a debt spiral that seems nearly unstoppable. The more into debt the federal government goes, the more it must spend on interest payments to service its debt. That pushes government spending upwards, because the government never cuts enough spending to account for the additional cost of paying its outstanding debts. That, in turn, leads to even more debt. In January 2025, the Congressional Budget Office estimated that in fiscal year 2025, the federal government will spend $952 billion on net interest related to its debts. In fiscal year 2026, it will surpass $1 trillion.[7] That's enough money to give every American close to $3,000 per year.[8]

Increased debt, deficits, and government spending on interest have put the U.S. economy in an extremely precarious situation. One of the most significant dangers is the growing threat to the U.S. dollar's status as the world's reserve currency. For decades, the dollar has enjoyed a privileged position in the global financial system. Because international trade, especially in vital commodities like oil, is largely conducted in dollars, and because central banks around the world hold U.S. dollars as a key reserve asset, America has been able to borrow at lower interest rates and run massive deficits without facing the kinds of currency crises that plague other nations. But that status is not guaranteed. If investors and foreign governments begin to believe that America does not intend to get its fiscal house in order, they could start shifting their reserves into other currencies or assets, undermining global demand for dollars and destabilizing the entire financial system.

If the dollar were to lose its reserve currency status, the consequences would be immediate and severe. Trillions of dollars currently held overseas, whether in central bank reserves, sovereign wealth funds, or private accounts, could come flooding back into the United States as foreign holders dump their greenbacks. That surge of returning dollars would dramatically increase the domestic money supply, triggering a wave of inflation unlike anything seen in modern U.S. history. And as the value of the dollar declines, foreign investors would rush to buy up American assets before their purchasing power falls further. Land, housing, farmland, natural resources, factories—virtually everything would be on the table. This influx of foreign capital might sound like a positive, but in reality it would mean Americans being outbid in their own cities and neighborhoods, losing control over strategically important assets, and watching their savings crash in value while foreign interests capitalize on the chaos.

That shift wouldn't happen overnight, but it could accelerate quickly once confidence disappears. And when demand for the dollar falls, its value drops: imports become more expensive, Americans' purchasing power diminishes, and inflation increases. Inflation is already a growing concern. In normal economic conditions, the Federal Reserve would respond to high inflation by raising interest rates, but with the national debt at $37 trillion and continuing to rise, interest rate hikes come at a heavy cost. Every percentage point increase in rates adds hundreds of billions of dollars in additional annual interest payments on the debt. The Fed is now operating under political and fiscal pressure not to raise rates too much, even when it might be necessary to curb inflation.

This creates a dangerous trap. If the Fed doesn't raise rates aggressively enough, inflation could spiral out of control, lowering the value of the dollar and further eroding trust in the U.S. financial system. However, if the Fed does raise rates significantly, the cost of servicing the debt could become so great that it consumes an ever-growing share of the federal budget, crowding out essential services, forcing higher taxes, or both. Either way, ordinary Americans lose, through higher prices, slower economic growth, a weaker currency, or reduced national stability.

Out-of-control debt threatens the foundations of America's economy and the prosperity of future generations. If we continue down the path we're on, the question is not if we'll face a crisis, but when and how bad it will be. Unless there are serious reforms, the weight of debt will eventually drag our entire nation under.

THE PERSONAL DEBT CRISIS

The federal government isn't the only one with a spending problem. American households have increased their levels of debt as well. Many years of low interest rates fueled debt spending for U.S. households, especially when prices rose sharply during the Biden presidency. Though interest rates have risen recently, they have come only after many years of abnormally low rates.

In 2025, *Forbes* reported that TransUnion, "one of the three biggest credit reporting agencies in the U.S., [said] the average credit card debt per American in May 2025 was $6,434."[9] In the same month, total consumer loan debt in the United States reached nearly $1.097 trillion, the highest figure ever recorded. Just one decade earlier, in May 2015, consumer loans totaled $634 billion; one decade before that, in May 2005, it was just $299 billion.[10]

Student loan debt has also become a significant problem for tens of millions of Americans. In 2006, total student loan debt was about $520 billion. By the end of 2024, it had reached $1.77 trillion, the highest number recorded to date. The Education Data Initiative reported in March 2025, "The average federal student loan debt balance is $38,375, while the total average balance (including private loan debt) may be as high as $41,618."[11] Debt from student loans weighs down millions of young and middle-aged people, keeping them from improving their financial situation and pursuing their dreams. Student loan debt, rather than a home mortgage, has become the largest monthly expense for many.

Auto loans are yet another area of serious concern. Using data from Experian, LendingTree reported in June 2025 that "Americans borrow an average of $41,720 for new vehicles and $26,144 for used vehicles." LendingTree further noted that "auto loan debt is the second-largest category behind mortgages. Overall, Americans owe $1.642 trillion in auto loan debt, according to the Federal Reserve Bank of New York, accounting for 9.0% of American consumer debt."[12]

These numbers clearly portray the reality: American families are drowning in debt. And as costs continue to rise, the problem will become only greater. Some studies and surveys have shown that more than 60 percent of American workers live from paycheck to paycheck.[13] When the economy enters its next employment downturn, millions (perhaps tens of millions) of families may be at risk of failing to make their debt payments, which could put lenders in a troubling position. If the problem is large enough, failure to make debt payments could result in widespread problems for the economy and financial system.

In the past, when such crises have occurred, the Federal Reserve and federal government have been eager to come to the rescue with new stimulus programs and bailouts. However, the current national debt crisis and growing inflation rates could force policymakers and the Fed to avoid taking such actions in a future crisis. The government simply might not be able to afford it.

HOUSING MARKET BUBBLE

Anyone who lived through the Great Recession of 2007–09 will tell you that a housing market crash on a wide scale can create crisis-level problems in other parts of the U.S. economy, especially the financial sector. Housing price indexes indicate that, as of mid-2025, America is likely in the midst of one of history's largest housing bubbles.[14]

A housing bubble is an economic condition characterized by a rapid and unsustainable increase in home prices, driven largely by speculation, excessive demand, and the widespread belief that housing values will continue to rise indefinitely. Easy credit, lax lending standards, and investor behavior, rather than underlying fundamentals (like income growth or housing supply), often fuel these price surges. Typically, the bubble bursts after prices peak, demand weakens, and home values plummet, leaving homeowners, banks, and investors with severe financial losses that can lead to even broader economic consequences.

During the height of the COVID-19 pandemic, the federal government and Federal Reserve injected an unprecedented amount of money into global markets, and much of this money ended up in the housing market. The M2 money supply over the past few years demonstrates this.

M2 is a broad measure of the money supply that includes liquid assets, such as physical currency, demand deposits, and other checkable deposits, and "near money" (slightly less liquid) assets, such as savings accounts, small-denomination time deposits (under $100,000), and retail money market mutual funds. Economists and policymakers use M2 to assess the total amount of money readily available in the economy for spending and investment. It is, therefore, a key indicator of potential inflationary pressure and overall monetary conditions.

According to the Federal Reserve Bank of St. Louis, the M2 money supply increased by $3.93 trillion in 2020 and another $2.45 trillion in 2021—unprecedented figures.[15] Since there was a surge in demand for housing at a time when most of the U.S. economy was closed or greatly affected by social distancing restrictions, much of the increase in the M2 money supply went into the housing market. (Housing sales price data reflects this.)

The average sales price of a home sold in the United States in the fourth quarter of 2019, just months before the start of the pandemic, was $384,600, as shown by figures from the U.S. Census Bureau and the U.S. Department of Housing and Urban Development. By the second quarter of 2022, prices had skyrocketed to $525,100, the largest and most rapid increase in U.S. history. Prices have stabilized since then, although the average is still above $500,000 as of mid-2025.[16]

The ratio of home price to income has also soared. From January 2009 to April 2020, the average home price in America was typically about five and a half times that of the median household income.[17] In other words, homes cost about 5.5 years' worth of the median household's earnings. In early 2022, during Biden's term, the ratio rose above seven for the first time ever, and it has remained above seven for most months since then.[18] (Before this, the only time the ratio approached seven was just prior to the 2007–09 housing crash.[19])

This not only shows how unaffordable purchasing a home has become. It also shows that sharp increases in the ratio of home prices to household incomes can signal a large housing market correction. If history is indicative of the future, the U.S. housing market should decline rapidly at some point before the end of 2028. That doesn't mean it will, but that's what the data suggests will happen.

WALL STREET OVERHEATING

American equities markets, such as the stock market, have also risen rapidly in the wake of the COVID-19 pandemic, as the U.S. housing sector has done. Take the S&P 500, for example. (The S&P 500 is a stock market index that measures the performance of five hundred of the largest U.S. companies across various industries. It is commonly used to gauge the health of the overall U.S. economy and stock market.) From January 2020, just prior to the pandemic, to the end of June 2025, the S&P 500 increased by more than 90 percent. That's one of the biggest increases ever recorded over a five-and-a-half-year period.[20]

In previous decades, when equities markets increased as quickly as they have in the past five years, it was common for a crash or large correction to follow. That's what happened during the burst of the dot-com bubble in the early 2000s, as well as during the Great Recession in 2007–09.[21]

It is possible that equities markets will continue to rise for years to come. However, there will be a correction eventually, and, based on the data we have available, it will likely be sooner rather than later.

The threat to America's financial system isn't only about inflated stock prices or speculative tech bubbles, though. It's also about what lies beneath the surface of Wall Street: the massive, complex, and often poorly understood derivatives market.

Derivatives are financial contracts whose value is based on the performance of an underlying asset, index, or interest rate. These assets can include futures, options, credit default swaps, and other instruments. In theory, derivatives can serve legitimate economic purposes, such as hedging risk or providing liquidity. For example, an airline might use oil futures to lock in fuel prices and protect itself against sudden spikes, or a market maker might sell options to ensure investors can easily buy or sell securities. But in practice, large financial institutions have often used them to amplify bets, obscure risk, or engage in highly leveraged speculation.[22] In other words, Wall Street often uses derivatives to *gamble*, and, like all gambling, derivatives can carry a significant amount of risk.

Derivatives are dangerous because of the size and inter-connectedness of the market. The derivatives market could be as large as $1 quadrillion. (Yes, you read that right—*quadrillion*.) Investopedia's J. B. Maverick notes, "Some market analysts even place the size of the [derivatives] market at more than 10 times that of the total world gross domestic product (GDP)."[23]

How could a market be so large? There are several reasons, but two in particular stand out.

First, derivatives are not the assets themselves but are based on underlying assets. Theoretically, there is practically no limit to the number of derivatives contracts that could be made.

To understand how this works, imagine a major football game is about to take place. You and your friends all place bets on the outcome—who wins, who scores first, total points, and so on. But then, other people start betting not just on the game but on your bets—whether your prediction will be right, how much you might win, whether someone else will cover your losses, and even on the outcome of those side bets. Soon, there are hundreds of layers of wagers stacked on top of a single football game, with thousands of people involved, most of whom have never even watched the teams play. If the final score comes out differently than expected, or if one big bettor can't pay up, the whole network of bets collapses, pulling everyone down with it.

The derivatives market on Wall Street is somewhat like that. A relatively small set of real-world assets—mortgages, bonds, currencies, or interest rates—sits at the bottom. Towering above it is a sprawling mountain of contracts, speculations, and counterparty obligations, and, as in the football-betting analogy above, it takes only one unexpected outcome or one failed player to set off a chain reaction that affects countless people involved.

A second reason the derivatives market is so large is that many derivatives contracts exist for speculative purposes rather than genuine hedging. In other words, traders and financial institutions are using derivatives not only to manage risk but also to make bets on the future direction of interest rates, stock prices, currencies, and countless other financial variables. These speculative trades often involve significant leverage, meaning that a relatively small amount of money can be used to control a much larger position. That leverage amplifies both potential gains and potential losses, encouraging more trading and more complex strategies.

Institutions create layer upon layer of derivatives, not because they are necessary to support real economic activity but because they offer a chance to generate quick profits. In many cases, dozens or even hundreds of derivatives contracts might be based on a single asset. The more complex the bets, the greater the number of contracts that are needed to offset potential risks, leading to exponential growth in the overall size of the market.

If you're not interested in trading derivatives (and I assume that most of you reading this book are not), then why should you care about them? You should care for the same reason that nearly all Americans suddenly cared about mortgage-backed securities during the height of the Great Recession: the risks created on Wall Street can impact the entire economy.

Financial institutions, including the biggest banks in America, are entangled in a large web of counterparty agreements. If one major player fails to meet its obligations, the impact can cascade through the entire system, triggering a chain reaction that can topple firms far removed from the original failure.

This is not just a theoretical concern. Derivatives played a central role in the 2008 financial crisis, when mortgage-backed securities and credit default swaps tied to subprime loans collapsed. At the time, even experienced economists and regulators didn't fully grasp the scale of the exposure or how it was able to spread so quickly. Today, even though there have been some regulatory reforms, many of the same vulnerabilities still exist.

The lack of transparency is one of the most troubling aspects of the derivatives market. While some derivatives are traded on regulated exchanges, a large portion are still traded over the counter, meaning they occur privately between institutions. That makes it very difficult for outsiders, including regulators, lawmakers, and even other financial firms, to know who holds what risk and how concentrated or dangerous that risk might be.

This opacity creates a false sense of security. On paper, everything might appear stable. But if market conditions suddenly shift because of a major default, a spike in interest rates, or a global economic shock, the hidden risks embedded in the derivatives market could quickly emerge, unleashing a crisis that spreads far beyond Wall Street.

And because derivatives are deeply intertwined with other parts of the economy (think pensions, insurance companies, and municipal finances), a major disruption could ripple through to retirement accounts, consumer credit markets, and even state and local governments.

This means that derivatives are a financial time bomb. As long as the system appears to be functioning smoothly, the risks remain hidden and largely ignored. But when the music stops, when liquidity dries up, when counterparties cannot pay, and when confidence vanishes, the results could be catastrophic.

America's economy is already under strain from debt, government spending, and asset bubbles. The derivatives market is an additional factor in that equation: perhaps the most dangerous part but the least visible, and so it remains largely out of the public conversation.

ARTIFICIAL INTELLIGENCE DISRUPTION

Artificial intelligence (AI) has the potential to usher in a new golden age for the United States. AI could discover a cure for cancer. It will certainly make many industries significantly more efficient, causing costs related to supplying and manufacturing goods and services to plummet. AI-driven automation could make the United States able to compete with global competitors in areas once thought to be impossible. Whole sectors of the economy could be transformed for the better. But along with all of these positive developments will come other kinds of costs, the most significant of which is job disruption.

As AI becomes more effective and eliminates more jobs currently done by humans, more parts of the U.S. job market will shrink. In the past, many analysts have assumed (wrongly, I think) that this will disproportionately harm lower-income workers in the service industry. The assumption was that kiosks and other kinds of automation would remove the need to have humans manning cash registers and flipping burgers. Although that will certainly be a problem, the impact on service workers will be far less problematic than the effect AI will have (and is already having) on knowledge-based, highly analytical roles, such as doctors, researchers, computer scientists, graphic designers, human resource workers, accountants, and business lawyers. Especially easy targets for replacement by AI will be any job that involves data entry; following formulaic steps; analyzing information and then coming to conclusions; or designing new versions of existing products or services.

In April 2025, *Forbes* contributor Jack Kelly noted,

Estimates vary, but experts converge on a transformative window of 10 to 30 years for AI to reshape most jobs. A McKinsey report projects that by 2030, 30% of current U.S. jobs could be automated, with 60% significantly altered by AI tools. Goldman Sachs predicts [that up to] 50% of jobs could be fully automated by 2045, driven by generative AI and robotics.[24]

But here's the catch: those tremendous economic gains from AI will not arrive all at once. They will come gradually and often in ways that will cause disruption before bringing improvement. The early stages of AI adoption will likely eliminate far more jobs than they create. That dynamic could lead to a sudden, sharp rise in unemployment across a wide array of industries, many of which are foundational to the American middle class.

What happens, for example, when the owner-operator truck driver who took out a $150,000 loan to buy a new rig is suddenly made obsolete by a fully autonomous trucking fleet?[25] What happens when he cannot find work, cannot make his loan payments, and defaults on his debt? And what happens when thousands, or even tens of thousands, of drivers face the same reality at the same time?

Now apply that same logic to call center employees, radiologists, paralegals, and junior software developers. What happens to the banks, credit unions, and auto lenders who extended loans to these workers, assuming they would have stable incomes for years to come? What happens when consumers stop spending because they are afraid that they could be next? What happens when mortgage payments, car payments, and credit card bills go unpaid—not because people are irresponsible but because their entire profession disappeared almost overnight?

The fallout from widespread AI-driven job losses could mirror the early stages of a financial crisis. Consumer spending could collapse. Loan defaults could increase. Banks could face mounting losses. Panic could spread throughout credit markets. And, with each passing week, confidence in the economy might deteriorate further.

If this disruption coincides with an already fragile economic moment—for example, high interest rates, elevated inflation, or a weakening housing market—the impact could be devastating. And with record national debt and limited financial tools available, policymakers' options for intervention could be much more limited than in past crises.

In theory, the United States will eventually reach a new economic equilibrium: new industries will emerge; some displaced workers will retrain or shift into new fields; AI will improve life in countless ways. However, the transition will likely be painful and protracted, and if it happens to coincide with another major crisis, it could be the spark that ignites the next great crash.

Technological progress can be a blessing, but poorly managed or poorly timed technological progress can also be the match that lights the fuse. AI is not guaranteed to cause an economic disaster—far from it—but its disruptive potential is real. For millions of Americans already living paycheck to paycheck, it might be one shock too many.

GLOBAL INSTABILITY AND CONFLICT

The United States is facing a number of geopolitical threats, in addition to the many economic indicators pointing to a large economic decline coming soon. America's economy is tied to the rest of the world more than ever before, which means that wars, pandemics, or other destabilizing events could have severe consequences on U.S. markets and American families.

In the past, the United States was able to weather regional conflicts and global instability with relatively minimal damage to its economy, but that is no longer the case. A truly globalized economy, coupled with America's ballooning national debt, weakened energy independence, and increasingly fragile supply chains, means that regional wars in Europe, Asia, or the Middle East can now affect the U.S. economy in a matter of days or even hours. In some cases, the effects can be felt instantaneously, especially in financial markets, commodity pricing, and currency fluctuations.

The war in Ukraine, for example, has shown how deeply interconnected global food and energy markets have become. Sanctions on Russia, one of the world's top energy and fertilizer producers, drove up prices across multiple sectors: oil prices surged as natural gas supplies to Europe were cut; global wheat and grain prices spiked. For countries such as the United States, which rely heavily on global commodity flows and trade routes, such disruptions translated into higher inflation, increased production costs, and additional pressure on working families, even though the conflict was occurring thousands of miles away.[26]

Imagine what might happen if a much larger conflict erupted.

Tensions between the United States and China continue to escalate, particularly over Taiwan. At the time of this writing in mid-2025, Chinese naval activity in the East and South China Seas has reached very high levels.[27] At the same time, the United States has been increasing its military support for Taiwan and strengthening defense partnerships across the Indo–Pacific region.[28] Most experts agree that a direct military conflict between China and Taiwan, especially one involving U.S. forces or weapons, would result in a global economic shock far greater than the one sparked by Russia's invasion of Ukraine.

Why? Because China, unlike Russia, is the world's second-largest economy, a global manufacturing hub, and the largest exporter on Earth. It also holds around $800 billion in U.S. Treasury securities.[29] A military confrontation with China would trigger market panic and cause immediate supply chain breakdowns, a collapse in global consumer confidence, surging prices for countless goods, and a flight to financial safety that would destabilize stock markets and potentially devalue the dollar.

Even without a war, a large-scale economic conflict with China, such as a trade war or mutual sanctions, could plunge both countries (and possibly the world) into recession. At the present, American businesses are still heavily reliant on Chinese factories, labor, and raw materials, so if U.S.-China connections are severed or even suspended, shortages could emerge across multiple industries. The United States might also face retaliatory actions from Beijing, such as restrictions on rare earth metals vital to manufacturing and defense, or a mass sell-off of U.S. debt.

The risk is not only from China. The Middle East remains a hotbed of instability, especially with tensions boiling over between Israel and its neighbors, and the possibility of broader regional conflict always looming. The world's economy continues to depend heavily on oil and gas from the region. Any disruption—whether from military conflict, terrorism, or political revolution—could send global energy prices soaring, reigniting inflation and undermining economic growth.

Then there are the wild cards: rogue cyberattacks, bioterrorism, pandemics, and political assassinations. We live in an era in which a relatively small number of bad actors can bring global markets to a halt with a well-timed attack: a cyber assault on a major energy grid; a shutdown of financial systems in London, Tokyo, or New York; a shipping blockade that delays food or medical supplies. These once-theoretical threats are now a real possibility for nation-states and non-state actors alike.

All of this adds up to one frightening truth: global instability is no longer something America can afford to ignore. Our economic system is so interdependent and overleveraged that a major crisis anywhere could become a major crisis everywhere, and because we are no longer fiscally or industrially self-sufficient, the United States is very vulnerable to external shocks, more so than it has been in decades.

Geopolitical conflict has always been a part of human history. However, in a world as complex, volatile, and digitally connected as ours, the consequences of a major global disruption could be more devastating than anything we have seen before, and, unfortunately, the odds of such a disruption occurring are growing.

TRIGGER EVENTS

As we've seen throughout history, it is rarely just one factor that creates the conditions for an economic crash. It occurs when existing weaknesses in the system—such as rising debt, inflated asset prices, and unsustainable speculation—are exposed suddenly, often by a single event or tipping point. That spark is what I call a "trigger event." It might seem small at first, and it might even appear unrelated to the financial system, but once it strikes, it sets off a chain reaction that ignites the powder keg beneath the surface.

There are many possible triggers. While no one knows which will set off the next crash, several highly plausible scenarios deserve close attention.

A Cyberattack on the Financial System and Critical Infrastructure

Imagine waking up on a Monday morning and discovering that your bank account is inaccessible. Your credit cards do not work. The

ATM near your house is out of service, and there are numerous news reports of a cyberattack targeting Wall Street's core infrastructure. This might sound like science fiction, but in recent years, U.S. intelligence agencies, academics, and cybersecurity experts have warned that hostile nation-states and well-funded criminal organizations are actively probing vital American systems for weaknesses.[30]

A successful cyberattack on the U.S. financial system could lock up markets, freeze critical financial functions, and destroy public confidence in digital banking. Even if the damage were only temporary, the panic it would unleash could cause an immediate run on banks, market sell-offs, and chaos in the payments system. If confidence in the integrity of digital transactions disappears, even for a short time, the modern economy could grind to a halt.

A Nuclear Terrorist Attack on a Major U.S. City

The use of a nuclear weapon on an American city is a terrifying scenario. As unsettling as it may be, national security experts take this threat seriously. In a single moment, tens or even hundreds of thousands of lives could be lost, and the economic consequences would be incalculable.

Markets could collapse overnight. Entire cities could be evacuated. The government might invoke martial law. Supply chains could be shattered, foreign investment could flee the United States, and global confidence in American security could vanish. The financial system, already straining under debt and overextension, could easily break under that kind of stress.

The Outbreak of Another Global Pandemic

The COVID-19 pandemic revealed how fragile our economy truly is. Despite living in one of the wealthiest and most advanced nations in the world, America was completely unprepared for the cascading effects of mass shutdowns, supply chain disruptions, and skyrocketing unemployment.

Now, imagine a virus that is even more contagious and deadly, or a bioterrorist-engineered pathogen deliberately released in airports or subways. In today's hyperconnected world, disease can spread faster than ever, and so can fear. A second global pandemic could trigger market shutdowns, force governments to print even more money, push millions more out of the workforce, and accelerate the kinds of inflation and labor disruptions we have already seen.

A Flash Crash in the Derivatives Market

The derivatives market is massive, opaque, and deeply interconnected. If the sudden failure of one major institution—perhaps due to miscalculated risk, bad data, reckless or irresponsible behavior, or a counterparty default—could ignite a global cascade of losses. Traders would rush to unwind positions, margin calls would go unmet, and because many derivatives are off-balance-sheet items, no one would know how bad the damage was until it was too late.

Think of it as a massive game of financial Jenga. Pull out the wrong block, and the entire tower comes crashing down—but unlike the children's game, this involves retirement savings, pensions, home loans, and the solvency of entire governments.

A Collapse in Commercial Real Estate

For decades, commercial real estate has been a pillar of the U.S. economy, supported by the steady demand for office buildings, retail space, and urban infrastructure. That foundation has begun to erode in the wake of the COVID-19 pandemic and the rise of remote work. Many cities now have entire office towers sitting empty, not temporarily but permanently. Companies are downsizing their physical footprints; malls are losing anchor tenants; urban commercial districts are struggling with rising vacancies, declining foot traffic, and falling property values.

This slow-moving crisis could quickly turn into a major financial shock. Commercial real estate loans are often bundled into securities and sold to investors, much like residential mortgages were prior to the 2008 crash. If enough property owners begin to default on those loans or if values fall too far too fast, the financial institutions holding those securities could face steep losses.[31]

Many banks, especially regional and midsize ones, are greatly affected by shifts in commercial real estate. A sudden drop in property values could trigger a wave of bank failures, leading to a credit crunch that ripples through the entire economy: small businesses could struggle to get loans; construction projects could stall; pension funds and insurance companies invested in commercial properties might face enormous losses. Unlike residential real estate, there is no obvious recovery plan if demand for commercial space continues to decline.[32]

The danger here is both economic and psychological. Empty buildings are visible signs of decay. They undermine confidence in cities, discourage new investment, and feed into the narrative that the economy is faltering. If enough people begin to believe that a collapse is underway, their behavior can help to make it a reality.

THE OPENING ACT

Terrified yet? If you are not worried, you likely aren't paying attention. The threats to our economy are real and growing. Although some progress has been made in recent months, the core issues remain: the next big crash is going to happen. It could happen soon, and when it does, it would be wise to be prepared.

The threats discussed in this chapter are just the opening act. The bigger issue facing the United States today—and the primary subject of this book—is that most Americans are not prepared for the fallout of the next big crash, let alone the crash itself. This is true even of many people who think they are prepared. The majority of Americans have no idea of what's coming.

Many of the world's largest financial institutions have been preparing, though, with the help of political allies in Washington and your state capital. They have been rewriting the rules so that when the next big crash happens, *they* will be protected—at the expense of *your* property rights, and, depending on how things shake out, *your* wealth, too.

In the next three chapters, we will examine two of the least understood and most dangerous threats hiding in plain sight: the Depository Trust Company, a private institution with unprecedented control over U.S. securities; and the growing push for programmable central bank digital currencies. These currencies promise government-controlled efficiency but risk transforming the dollar into a mechanism of surveillance and control.

I will present the people behind these systems and proposals for the future. We'll follow the money. I'll show how regulatory loopholes and political incentives have created a perfect storm that could rob you of your financial freedom in a single news cycle. We'll also examine evidence that suggests—though does not prove definitively—that the CIA and other government agencies and officials may be involved in some of these efforts and how their involvement could put you and your family in extreme economic danger.

In the final chapter, I will outline the game plan that I am following to prepare for the potential crises described in this book.

These are difficult concepts to discuss, but I hope you will agree that it is essential to pay attention. You may end up overpreparing for a crisis that never occurs—but it is certainly better than being caught unprepared in the midst of a massive economic catastrophe.

So, buckle up. It's going to be a wild ride.

2

HOW WALL STREET RIGGED U.S. INVESTMENTS, AND WHY YOU COULD LOSE EVERYTHING IN THE NEXT BIG CRASH

I magine waking up one morning to discover that everything you thought you owned—your retirement savings, your stock portfolio, your children's college funds—wasn't really yours. Not legally. Not in any way that matters when the system is crashing.

This is not the plot of a dystopian novel or the fever dream of a fringe conspiracy theorist. It is the reality of modern finance, embedded in the wiring of today's securities markets and concealed by legal jargon and red tape.

Over the past half century, American investors, large and small, have had their property rights systematically removed. The stated goals were efficiency and innovation, but the public was not consulted, and many lawmakers had little grasp of the consequences when they helped Wall Street firms impose these changes. Those who benefited most—large commercial banks and global financial institutions—did not care to explain the changes to ordinary investors. Ordinary investors, for the most part, were left in the dark.

A fuse has been quietly wired into our financial system. When the fuse ignites and the next financial crisis hits (and it will, whether it comes in six months or six years), the question won't be, "How much did I lose?" It will be, "Why wasn't I told that I never owned it in the first place?"

To grasp how we got here and why the next crash could be unlike anything we've experienced, it's necessary to understand three things: the Uniform Commercial Code, the Depository Trust Company, and the uncomfortable truth about securities ownership in America. These are the keystones of our system, the system that quietly rewrote the fundamental rules of financial ownership.

In this chapter, I'll explain how the public was sold a lie. I'll describe how Wall Street, government regulators, and allied institutions such as the Uniform Law Commission and American Law Institute engineered a fragile system that enriches and protects the powerful while putting everyday investors at extraordinary risk. Finally, I plan to show you why this problem must be addressed before it's too late.

This is a tale of deception that, like it or not, you and many of the people you love have been dragged into. The Big Lie—the part almost no one is told—is that most Americans do not directly own the securities investments that they believe are theirs. When the system buckles, it is unlikely that Wall Street gamblers will pay the price. Instead, it will likely be every retiree, every parent saving for college, and every worker who thought their nest egg was safe.

THE BIG LIE

How many stocks, bonds, exchange-traded funds, and other securities investments do you own? What do other members of your family own? I know the answer, believe it or not, and it is not a guess. I can tell you *exactly* how many securities you and everyone you know own, because the answer is the same for nearly everyone who lives in America. The answer is zero. Most people and institutions are *not* the registered owners of stocks, bonds, or other securities, regardless of how much they have invested.

You may be thinking, "This is insane. This cannot possibly be correct." You can log in to your brokerage account and see your 401(k) statements. You may have purchased an investment product recently and seen your name on it, along with a list of investments and dollar amounts. How can it be true that you are not the direct owner of those securities?

The key thing to understand is that what you think you own are essentially *contracts*: they provide financial and legal benefits tied to those investments. These contracts are called security entitlements. Later in this chapter, I will explain in more detail how security entitlements work. The simple fact is, though, if you looked up the registered owner of an investment you think you own, it would not show your name. It's similar to the difference between leasing a car and actually owning the car. Many people do not understand that "owning" securities is actually more like leasing.

This becomes especially important when thinking about the next big economic crash. Since you don't directly own your investments, the usual legal protections are far weaker than most people realize, because you aren't the registered owner and don't possess the securities.

So, here's the trillion-dollar question: if you aren't the direct, registered owner of your investments, then who is? You might guess it's your broker: if you buy a hundred shares of Coca-Cola through Fidelity or Merrill Lynch, is your broker the registered owner? Again, no.

The true registered owner of most securities in America is a little-known financial institution called the Depository Trust Company, or DTC. In 2025, DTC reported holding more than 1.4 million active securities worth $87.1 trillion, an amount so large it is difficult for me to fathom.[33] For comparison, the entire U.S. federal budget in 2024 was $6.8 trillion, less than a tenth of what is handled by DTC.

In the early 1970s, a group of major financial institutions and a man named William Dentzer created DTC, with the stated purpose of making securities transactions more efficient and less costly. I'll give more of Dentzer's background in a later chapter, but here's a brief overview. Dentzer had ties to U.S. intelligence and was connected with some very wealthy and influential Americans. He did not have experience in the financial industry, yet he was installed as chairman of DTC, which became one of the most powerful institutions on Wall Street. As you'll see, there were likely other motivations at play beyond simply enhancing efficiency.

DTC is a subsidiary of the Depository Trust & Clearing Corporation (DTCC), the parent company that dominates the U.S. clearing and settlement system.[34] (DTCC also owns other clearing entities, like the National Securities Clearing Corporation and the Fixed Income Clearing Corporation.[35])

DTC has a nominee partnership called Cede & Co., which is the name that appears on issuer records as the registered owner of securities. Through this nominee partnership, DTC holds the vast majority of U.S. stocks, bonds, and other securities in pooled form on behalf of DTCC's "participants." The primary DTCC participants are large banks and brokers, such as Merrill Lynch and Fidelity.[36] Cede & Co. is the registered owner of record, and DTC controls and operates Cede.[37]

Here's a short summary: banks and brokers own DTCC; DTCC owns DTC; DTC controls Cede; and Cede's name sits on the securities. In practice, that means the institutions that run Wall Street are the true registered owners of the securities you think you own. Since DTCC is a corporation owned by its participant institutions, i.e., they hold shares in DTCC,[38] the system is a closed loop. The majority of individuals, such as you and me, can't even become owners of the company that holds our securities, because DTCC isn't publicly traded.

The fact that most people don't directly own the securities tied to their investments is a significant problem, since without registered ownership, your rights are whatever is laid out in the law or in your security entitlement contract (the only thing about your securities that you do own). This arrangement means that Wall Street can control and use your securities to generate profits without your knowledge or consent, while leaving you with little more than an account statement.

When I first heard about DTC and the centralization of nearly all of America's securities investments, I thought that the researchers explaining it to me had lost touch with reality. How could something so significant have slipped past me? I consulted a former investment banker and a board member of public and private companies, i.e., a Wall Street expert. This individual is a consultant to high-powered CEOs, a highly successful investor, and a *New York Times* bestselling author.[39]

I shared the notes and explanations I had collected from other researchers. Then I asked my friend directly whether it was true that direct ownership of securities has mostly been taken away from individual investors and businesses.

"Is what I'm hearing about securities ownership and DTC true?" I asked. "And if so, how many people on Wall Street know this? How has DTC managed to keep this a secret?"

"Justin," my friend said, "everyone on Wall Street knows this."

Everyone on Wall Street knows this.

My investor friend was right. Many people have never heard of DTC, DTCC, or their subsidiaries, but if you know where to look, it's easy to verify that investors don't directly own their securities. The U.S. Securities and Exchange Commission (SEC) states it openly.

Here's how the SEC's Office of Investor Education and Advocacy describes the system:

> Most large U.S. broker-dealers and banks are DTC participants, meaning that they deposit and hold securities at DTC. DTC appears in an issuer's stock records as the sole registered owner of securities deposited at DTC. DTC holds the deposited securities in "fungible bulk," meaning that there are no specifically identifiable shares directly owned by DTC participants. Rather, each participant owns a pro rata interest in the aggregate number of shares of a particular issuer held at DTC. Correspondingly, each customer of a DTC participant, such as an individual investor, owns a pro rata interest in the shares in which the DTC participant has an interest.[40]

The SEC's explanation makes it clear, despite the industry jargon, that DTC's participants, such as stockbrokers and banks, do not actually own the securities held by DTC. DTC is the sole registered owner. What participants have instead is a *pro rata* interest, which is Latin for "in proportion."[41] In other words, participants don't own specific shares; they own contractual rights to a slice of the overall pie, i.e., the pool of stocks, bonds, or other securities held by DTC. Individual investors, like you, have only a pro rata interest in your *broker's* pro rata interest.

For example, a large investor that buys 11 percent of a company's stock is not the direct owner of those shares. It holds contractual rights to their broker-dealer's slice of that stock held by DTC. The broker-dealer, in turn, has only a proportional claim within DTC's pool. The sole registered owner remains DTC.[42]

If your head is spinning, you're not alone. Even those who know about DTC rarely talk about it, because the system is deliberately complex. The essential facts, though, are simple: you are not the direct, registered owner of your investments, including your stocks, bonds, or exchange-traded funds. DTC is the owner and, through its parent DTCC, is owned by powerful banks, broker-dealers, and other massive financial institutions. The rights you as an individual have to those investments are outlined in the fine-print clauses in security entitlement contracts (that many investors never read) and in government rules and laws (that many investors do not realize exist).

It's tempting to think that a system this complex must be as old as Wall Street itself, but it isn't. The DTC and its security entitlement framework are relatively new in American history and have overturned centuries of property law. Before DTC was created, investors enjoyed direct ownership of their securities and far greater legal protection. Those rights did not disappear by accident. Lawmakers in all fifty states, with the encouragement of Wall Street and other institutions, systematically dismantled them.

SETTING THE STAGE

Prior to the 1970s, it was common for investors to directly own the securities they purchased. Many even had the proof in hand; some of you may still remember stock certificates arriving in the mail with your name on them. The reason that no longer happens is simple: investors are no longer the registered owners of those stocks.

The old model maximized the rights of investors, but it is important to acknowledge that it did have some drawbacks. The process of transferring ownership of securities, such as stocks, was slow, burdensome, and paper-intensive. As trading volume grew in the 1960s, Wall Street had difficulty keeping up with demand and began searching for a more streamlined system.

That's where the DTC comes in. Created by banks and brokers in the early 1970s, DTC became a centralized vault for paper securities. By holding certificates in one place, brokers could settle trades by adjusting their internal ledgers, with no complex transfer of physical documents required. Buying and selling became as easy as moving names around on paper.

As technology improved, Wall Street realized it could go further: digitizing records, consolidating control, cutting costs, and opening new revenue streams. For this transition to occur, however, state laws and federal regulations needed to change.

In the 1970s, an initial round of amendments to Article 8 of the Uniform Commercial Code (UCC) laid the groundwork for a massive transformation of Wall Street's securities system. The UCC is a uniform state law that governs commercial transactions nationwide. (It has been adopted by all fifty states and certain federal jurisdictions, starting with Pennsylvania in 1952.) UCC Article 8 focuses specifically on investment securities.[43] These initial changes to UCC Article 8 made it easier for the newly created DTC to operate efficiently by providing the legal foundation for the indirect holding system.

The story doesn't end there. In the 1990s, due to influence from major financial institutions and the Uniform Law Commission (which I will explain more later in this chapter), lawmakers made another round of large-scale changes to UCC Article 8 that were even more consequential. These revisions gave priority over investors in certain bankruptcy situations to Wall Street's biggest financial players (particularly the "too big to fail" banks that were acting as secured creditors).

These amendments ensured that if a broker-dealer collapses after using customer securities as collateral for its own borrowing, the broker's secured creditors are legally first in line, outranking the very investors whose assets were pledged.[44] This change redefined what it means to "own" a security. Every state adopted these amendments between 1994 and 2001.

This isn't just my interpretation. It's written directly into the UCC. Article 8, Section 503(a) states that securities held by your broker "are not property of the securities intermediary, and are not subject to claims of creditors of the securities intermediary, *except as otherwise provided in Section 8-511*"[45] (italics added). That exception clause is critical. Section 8-511(b) stipulates that a broker's secured creditor with "control over the financial asset" has "priority over claims of the securities intermediary's entitlement holders."[46]

In plain English, if your broker pledges your securities as collateral and that pledge gives the bank legal control of them, the bank takes priority over your securities—even though you paid for them.

Article 8's redefinition of ownership hinges on the security entitlement concept mentioned earlier: it was, at the time, a new form of "property right" that has now become the near-universal standard for holding securities. This novel construct overturned centuries of common-law tradition. It replaced true ownership with a mere contractual claim against a middleman. It eliminated direct, registered ownership for virtually all ordinary investors. In the current structure, an individual claim exists only if the intermediary is solvent and compliant.

Think about what that means. The reason you don't have direct, registered ownership rights to the investments you've paid for is because legislators and governors in every state took those rights away—quietly, without your knowledge. There was no public debate, nor was there any meaningful informed consent.

These changes occurred decades ago, long before most current legislators entered politics. When I've explained to current state lawmakers that their constituents do not actually own their securities investments, most had no idea it was true. They were just as angry about it as many of you may be right now.

These revisions were not routine technical updates to improve commerce, and they were never intended to be. James Rogers, the law professor who served as principal drafter (reporter) of the Article 8 revisions, later described the 1990s project to revise UCC Article 8 as "Armageddon planning" for the financial system.[47] The revisions were intentionally designed to ensure market continuity and stability in the event of a catastrophic collapse.

However, the central justification for stripping investors of their direct property rights (the claim that prior law posed serious systemic risk) had little concrete foundation. Rogers explained later, "Somewhat to my surprise, I found that, although there were many general expressions to the effect that prior law did not provide a sufficiently certain legal framework for transactions implemented through the modern securities holding system, there was relatively very little specific description of the problems."[48]

One of Rogers's fellow drafters, law professor Paul Shupack, described it even more directly. In a 1995 memorandum to the Uniform State Laws Committee of the New York City Bar Association, Shupack wrote, "The conclusion that current law creates serious risk of systemic market failure is the SEC's, not mine. I have no basis independent of the SEC studies upon which to form a judgment about the empirical claim that drastic reform of Prior Article 8 is needed."[49] The SEC studies that Shupack referenced were never revealed.

To summarize, there was no clear, independently verified evidence that drastic reforms were necessary; yet it was deemed necessary to sacrifice investors' property rights in the name of systemwide financial stability.

Why, then, were these sweeping changes pushed through in every state? As several experts have documented, the primary beneficiaries were the largest financial institutions, which no longer had to bear the full brunt of failure. The system ensured that in a crisis, those institutions could be made whole first, by making customer securities part of the legal collateral pool. In effect, Wall Street's fail-safe came in the form of your investments.

You don't have to take my word for this. Several independent legal scholars reviewed the Article 8 revisions process and came to the same conclusions. Writing contemporaneously, they described how collusive financial interests shaped the law to their advantage, sidelined the investing public, and shifted risk away from large financial institutions and onto ordinary investors.

What follows may get a little dense, but bear with me—this is important, and these accounts show just how deliberately the system was tilted against you.

Kathleen Patchel, a law professor and widely regarded expert on the UCC legislative process, wrote that "[i]nterest groups, and bank lobbies in particular, were prime players in determining the fate of the Uniform Commercial Code as it moved through the state legislatures. The experience of the Code . . . is that a powerful business lobby like the banking industry can and will block a uniform law that does not meet its expectations."[50] The result, she warned, is a system "almost custom-made for the creation and enactment of pro-business legislation."[51] To illustrate the problem, Patchel cited the blunt assessment of one prominent UCC drafter and advocate, who likened the process to "appointing a committee of dogs to draw up a protective ordinance for cats."[52]

Patchel cautioned that when legislation purports to represent the "best" solution to a problem, the question becomes "Best for whom?"[53] When it came to Article 8, the answer was clear.

Francis Facciolo, a securities law professor who analyzed the revisions in detail, wrote that the drafting history "shows the considerable influence that a cohesive interest group can have":[54] in this case, the Wall Street financiers and other industry leaders who stood to gain the most from the law. He pointed to the evolution of the Article 8 revisions, as well as what he explicitly termed "collusion," as evidence of "the progressive watering down during the drafting process of protections granted to individual investors."[55] In short, bank lobbyists had enormous sway over the UCC revision process and ensured that the law bent to their interests.

Facciolo noted that the end result was not only a weaker set of investor safeguards but a fundamental shift in the very nature of what investors think they own. Citing the drafting committee's own official comments, he observed that revised Article 8 "creates a new type of property interest that 'is not a claim to a specific identifiable thing; [rather] it is a package of rights and interests that a person has against the person's securities intermediary and the property held by the intermediary.'"[56] In practice, as noted earlier, this means an investor's "ownership" exists only as a set of claims against their broker, not as ownership of the asset itself. This structure, in Facciolo's words, makes it "extremely unlikely that an investor in the indirect holding system will ever be able to prove that he or she has any interest in any particular financial asset."[57]

Facciolo revealed how Article 8 rewrote the very definition of ownership. Commercial law scholar Russell Hakes focused on why this legal shift in the definition of ownership leaves investors virtually powerless in practice.

Hakes wrote that under the new framework, an entitlement holder has "only extremely limited rights in the financial asset against persons other than its securities intermediary" and "no rights against the issuer of the financial asset."[58] He noted that those rights (which investors no longer have, due to the Article 8 amendments) represent "the essence of a property interest."[59] In other words, an investor's claims stop at their broker, with no direct recourse up the chain. In practice, Hakes warned that "it is an extraordinarily rare circumstance in which an entitlement holder's rights will be enforceable against a purchaser,"[60] making recovery of assets in a broker's failure exceptionally difficult.

Hakes was clear about who benefits: Wall Street. The revised rules, he wrote, "favor secured lenders to the securities industry in virtually every instance."[61] While he admitted that these preferences "facilitate much needed credit," Hakes warned that they do so by "shifting the risk of intermediary misbehavior almost entirely onto entitlement holders" and "go further than necessary."[62] The source of that "unnecessary risk," he argued, "appears to be . . . over-zealousness on the part of the securities industry in establishing a legal scheme to protect its lenders."[63]

In essence, the system shifted to insulate financial institutions, while the ordinary investors whose assets keep the system running must absorb the impact when things fall apart.

The revised Article 8, as Facciolo underscored, "includes major changes that should be of concern to all individual investors in America's securities markets," and "without significant amendments . . . individual investors will be profoundly disadvantaged."[64] His warnings, however, went largely ignored, as did those of other legal scholars. The law remained unchanged, and for decades the investing public had no idea how vulnerable they really were.

Only in the past few years has serious attention returned to Article 8, with a growing chorus calling for the reforms that should have been made three decades ago. Few people have captured the consequences of Article 8 more clearly than Jack McPherrin, one of the country's leading researchers on the UCC elimination of property rights. (I've worked closely with McPherrin for years on this and other issues; his research has informed much of what you've read so far in this chapter.)

McPherrin recently authored a publication for lawmakers, laying out the core dangers of Article 8 in plain terms. His analysis distills the problem succinctly:

> Ultimately, the changes to UCC Article 8 replaced ownership with a fragile contractual claim and force ordinary American investors to shoulder the full risk burden when things go wrong. Investors no longer own their securities. When a broker pledges customer assets as collateral for its own borrowing, those securities are immediately exposed. If that broker goes bankrupt, its secured creditors—typically the largest banks—take priority over the very investors whose capital fuels Wall Street's profits. In those circumstances, Article 8's priority rules ensure investors are treated as unsecured creditors—even when their broker has acted illegally and the investors themselves are entirely blameless.
>
> In a systemic crash involving cascading broker failures, the system would function exactly as designed: everyone but the investor would be made whole first. And if the crisis is severe enough, millions of Americans could see their life savings siphoned into the coffers of Wall Street's biggest banks.[65]

As McPherrin, leading legal scholars, and even the law's own drafters have made clear, the revisions to Article 8 were never about neutral modernization and efficiency. They were about crisis planning. They were about ensuring that when the next financial "Armageddon" comes, the system survives, while individual investors are sacrificed.

Put simply, the revisions rewrote the rules of ownership to serve Wall Street first. They shifted risk away from the largest financial institutions and onto families, retirees, and small businesses. A law that should have protected investors instead made them expendable. This means that if Wall Street is hit with cascading broker insolvencies during the next big crash, banks will be made whole first, while ordinary Americans could lose everything.

What makes this even more troubling is how it happened. These changes were driven by a coordinated influence campaign from Wall Street's largest financial institutions and their allies. They were pushed through quietly, in every state, without meaningful debate or public awareness. Legislators signed off on amendments they barely understood, while insiders assured them it was all necessary to reduce "systemic risk," an unsubstantiated claim. "Trust the experts," lawmakers were told, or as Facciolo put it, "Father knows best."[66]

The result is a system that has redefined ownership. You do not have full control over your investments; rather, your securities are controlled by the Depository Trust Company and owned by Cede & Co. What once was a direct property right is now a fragile contractual claim against your broker: a security entitlement. If your broker fails and your assets are swept into its collateral pool as it fights to survive, your life savings could vanish overnight, and you will have little recourse.

FAKE CONSUMER PROTECTIONS

Wall Street lawyers may protest that it's not as bad as it sounds. Regulations such as the SEC's Customer Protection Rule (Rule 15c3-3) generally require brokers to segregate customer investment securities from their own and prohibit using them as collateral in brokers' lending agreements.[67] In theory, that means your stocks, bonds, and other securities should be safe from seizure in a crash.

There are important exceptions, such as if you have a margin account, which is a brokerage account that lets you borrow from your broker to buy more investments than you could with cash alone. For example, you might put in $1,000 of your own cash and borrow another $1,000 from the broker, giving you $2,000 to invest. This is called buying on margin: it can potentially increase your gains, but it also magnifies your risk. Millions of people use margin accounts. (Now you may be wondering, "Are my investments safe if I avoid using a margin account?" The answer is no.)

Two major assumptions underpin the idea that existing regulations will protect investors from catastrophe. The first assumption is that regulators won't change the rules in the event of a disastrous economic crash. The second assumption is that Wall Street firms and banks are following the rules today and will keep doing so even when their survival is on the line. Neither assumption is realistic or historically accurate.

Let's look at the first assumption: the belief that the rules themselves are untouchable. In a major crash, the political pressure on Washington to prop up Wall Street would be enormous. Regulators could authorize brokerages to use customers' securities as collateral or direct the DTC to make more of its pooled securities available for loans, and there would be nothing you could do to stop it, because you have substantially reduced rights in the investments you bought. Remember, you're not the direct owner.

Under current U.S. law, policymakers could dismantle these so-called protections almost overnight if a major crash threatened the stability of the financial system. Here are a few of the most direct ways this could be done:

1. **Emergency suspension of SEC rules:** The SEC has authority under Exchange Act §12(k)(2) to "alter, supplement, suspend, or impose" rules in a declared emergency for up to ten business days, to "maintain or restore fair and orderly securities markets."[68] This power has been exercised in past crises, such as after the September 11 attacks in 2001 and during the 2008 financial panic.[69,70] The SEC could use it to relax or override

parts of the Customer Protection Rule (Rule 15c3-3), which normally requires brokers to keep fully paid customer securities segregated and out of reach for their own borrowing needs.

2. **Presidential emergency powers:** Under the International Emergency Economic Powers Act (IEEPA),[71] which can be invoked only following a national emergency declaration under the National Emergencies Act,[72] the president can block or regulate transactions and property involving "critical national assets" or foreign interests. These powers are most often used to impose economic sanctions on foreign governments, banks, and individuals (and they are exercised frequently for this purpose).[73] These powers were intended for international policy, but the IEEPA has been interpreted broadly enough that it could also be applied to assets inside the United States if they are connected to a foreign party or interest.[74] For example, in a systemic crisis linked to a cyberattack from a terrorist organization or hostile state, the president could restrict the transfer of securities held at the DTC and/or require that they be routed through a government-controlled stabilization mechanism for use by failing institutions.

3. **Creation of a securities stabilization authority:** Congress could enact an emergency "securities stabilization" framework, modeled on the Orderly Liquidation Authority (OLA) created by Title II of the Dodd-Frank Act.[75] This would not be an extension of any current power; it would have to be newly authorized by statute, just as OLA was in 2010. Once created, such a framework could empower a designated agency, such as the FDIC or the SEC, to direct the DTC and other clearing agencies to transfer, pool, or impose "haircuts" on securities

positions, reallocating a portion to distressed institutions or a federally controlled stabilization fund.

Each of these scenarios has either an existing statutory basis or a well-established procedural precedent that Congress could draw upon quickly in a crisis. The above list is far from exhaustive; there are other emergency powers, such as those held by the Federal Reserve, that could be invoked under crisis conditions. (I will explain more about these later in this chapter.)

Congress, of course, could go even further. In a genuine financial emergency (or the appearance of one), Congress could pass almost any law it deemed "necessary and proper" to protect the system. When the stakes are high enough, sweeping legislative measures have historically faced little immediate resistance and have been enacted quickly, such as with the 2008 Troubled Asset Relief Program bailout and the 2020 CARES Act, among many other examples.

The fact is that the safety net of protective regulations exists only as long as policymakers keep it in place—and in a crisis, their priority won't be you. History has shown that when financial stability is at risk, lawmakers and regulators have taken extraordinary measures to protect too-big-to-fail institutions.

Government intervention isn't the only threat. As I explained in the previous section, even without any new federal action, existing laws and structures underpinning the modern securities-holding system are heavily weighted in favor of large institutional creditors, leaving investors exposed.

That brings us to the second flawed assumption: that Wall Street will follow the rules when its survival is at stake. History suggests otherwise. In past crises, firms have improperly tapped customer assets without permission, preventing customers from recovering their property for several years. The following cases—spanning securities, commodities, and futures—show how customer protections that were supposed to be absolute collapsed in the moment of crisis, with supposedly "segregated" customer property siphoned away or frozen.

Lehman Brothers (2008)

When Lehman Brothers collapsed on September 15, 2008, it quickly became clear that much of the firm's customer property was not sitting safely in segregated accounts, as required. Instead, portions of it had been drawn into Lehman's own financing chain (either pledged to its clearing bank, JPMorganChase, or frozen mid-settlement in Wall Street's central clearing system), leaving customers locked out of their assets.

An investigation by the U.S. Commodity Futures Trading Commission found that for at least twenty-two months prior to Lehman's collapse, JPMorgan had been extending credit to Lehman for Lehman's proprietary transactions based in part on balances from customer accounts, exposing these accounts to Lehman's survival needs.[76] This arrangement meant that when Lehman filed for bankruptcy, JPMorgan could (and did) assert a lien over those balances. The bank froze roughly $333 million in customer accounts, holding them for approximately two weeks before the balances were transferred as part of the emergency sale of Lehman's brokerage operation to Barclays.[77]

Meanwhile, the Depository Trust and Clearing Corporation, the parent company of the Depository Trust Company, canceled and reversed about $468 million in transactions that were in process when the bankruptcy hit, pulling those customer assets back into Lehman's bankruptcy estate. A court order in February 2009 reversed DTCC's action, but by that point, customers had been without their property for nearly five months.[78]

These initial high-profile freezes were only part of the problem.

Although more than 110,000 accounts were transferred within weeks to other brokers, many other accounts totaling billions of dollars remained tied up in the bankruptcy estate for years as secured creditors asserted claims on the customer assets that Lehman improperly pledged. Final distributions to many of Lehman's customers did not even begin until June 7, 2013, nearly five years after Lehman's failure.[79]

Sentinel Management Group (2007)

The collapse of Sentinel Management Group in 2007 illustrates how quickly "segregated" customer assets can be pulled into a firm's own debts. Despite federal law requiring the Chicago-based investment manager to keep client securities separate, Sentinel had been commingling customer assets with company property and pledging them as collateral to the Bank of New York for a revolving credit line that reached as high as $500 million.[80]

When Sentinel declared bankruptcy in August 2007, the Bank of New York asserted a secured lien on collateral that included approximately $312 million in customer property, blocking customers from accessing significant portions of their portfolios.[81,82] The legal battle to free those assets lasted nearly a decade. In 2013, a federal appeals court ruled the bank should have known the assets were being used improperly,[83] and in 2016, the court finally voided the bank's claim.[84] Only then, nearly nine years after Sentinel's collapse, were customer assets finally able to be distributed back to their rightful owners.

MF Global (2011)

MF Global's collapse in October 2011 represents another example of a Wall Street firm raiding customer accounts to cover its own survival, in flagrant violation of existing customer protection rules. In its final days, facing a liquidity crisis triggered by bad bets on European sovereign debt, MF Global unlawfully tapped hundreds of millions of dollars from customer segregated accounts to meet margin calls and other obligations and filed false segregation reports.[85] By the time regulators intervened, more than $1.6 billion in customer property was missing.[86]

Because MF Global commingled these funds with its own (and, in many cases, transferred them to other banks and counterparties), they became tied up in bankruptcy until they could be traced and recovered. The shortfall left tens of thousands of customers, including farmers, ranchers, small businesses, and institutional traders, unable to access their assets and/or the liquidity they depended on for daily operations.[87] Although the bankruptcy trustee ultimately recovered enough to pay all allowed customer claims in full, the process took years. The first interim customer distribution didn't begin until April 2012,[88] and the last distribution was not completed until 2014, nearly two and a half years after the collapse.[89]

In the cases of Lehman, Sentinel, MF Global, and many others, a pattern is unmistakable: existing "customer protections," which were supposed to be absolute, failed. Customers discovered that "segregated" property was, in fact, not. They discovered that the wall protecting their assets from a failing firm's creditors was far thinner than the rules led them to believe.

Your securities investments, the culmination of years of saving and planning, would be far safer if you were their registered owner. But you're not. In the modern indirect holding system, most U.S. securities live in pooled, "street name" accounts at the DTC, legally titled to its nominee, Cede & Co. You are credited as a "beneficial owner" on an intermediary's books (not the outright owner). Under the revised Uniform Commercial Code Article 8, if your broker pledges your securities as collateral—even improperly—and a secured creditor gains "control," that creditor takes priority over what you believed to be your assets.[90] Your contractual claim to the securities falls to the back of the line in bankruptcy proceedings. You are treated not as the owner of specific property but as an unsecured creditor, and you must fight a protracted legal battle to claw back the assets you purchased.

This legal architecture explains the connecting theme in the case studies. In a crisis scenario, when a firm uses customer assets to buy itself time, your property can be frozen or tied up indefinitely. Even if you are eventually made whole, you can be locked out for years—missing price gains and dividends, losing the time value of money, and, most painfully of all, being denied liquidity when you need it most. Retirees, institutions, and small businesses that depend on daily access can be left stranded while markets rebound without them.

Many industry advocates and policymakers hold up the eventual return of assets in these cases as proof that the system works. In reality, a "victory" that leaves customers without access to their property for months or years—whether through a market rebound or an economic crisis—is not a victory. It's a failure. The delays, losses, and uncertainty are a built-in feature of a system designed to prioritize the stability of large institutions over the rights of individual investors. Ultimately, the "protections" that Wall Street firms and UCC advocates point to are often worth very little.

It wasn't always this way. Up until the 1970s, most investors held physical stock certificates in their own name, with strong, traditional property rights under the Fifth and Fourteenth Amendments. Clear title meant that if someone tried to take your shares, you had the full weight of constitutional protections behind you. That changed when Wall Street and lawmakers replaced direct registration with today's fully intermediated book-entry system. The shift centralized legal ownership under DTC and replaced firm property rights with fragile contractual claims (claims subject to the whims of regulators and intermediaries with a history of bending or breaking the rules when survival is on the line).

The cases described above are not even close to the worst-case scenario. The examples I've given were single-firm failures in a system that remained largely functional. In a cascading crash (several major intermediaries failing one after another), clearing utilities may halt or reverse transfers to protect the system, secured creditors could seize larger pools of assets, and bankruptcy courts would be overwhelmed. In the name of stability, regulators and policymakers could also invoke emergency powers to suspend already weak customer protection rules, override contractual claims, or redirect customer assets outright. In that world, "eventual recovery" becomes far less plausible, and whatever practical protections there are for the individual investor could vanish overnight.

To summarize, your property rights have been replaced with a contract. A constitutional guarantee has been replaced by a weak promise. When the next crisis comes, the odds will shift even further against you.

WHO'S REALLY IN CHARGE HERE?

Centralizing securities ownership introduces another set of dangers for everyday investors. Remember: individuals are not the direct, registered owners of most investment securities; legal title rests with the DTC, a subsidiary of DTCC, which in turn is owned by its participant shareholders, mainly large banks and Wall Street firms. However, DTC and its parent company are not the only players in the system. Because DTC is one of the most heavily regulated financial entities in the world, government regulators exercise a tremendous amount of control over Americans' securities.

The Depository Trust Company operates under multiple layers of oversight:

- As a covered clearing agency, DTC must follow rules issued by the Securities and Exchange Commission.[91]
- Under Title VIII of the Dodd-Frank Act, DTC is designated a systemically important financial market utility (SIFMU), which makes it subject to heightened federal oversight by the Federal Reserve and other regulators.[92]
- And, as a limited purpose trust company under New York law, DTC is also regulated by the New York State Department of Financial Services.[93]

Taken together, these designations give federal and state regulators varying degrees of authority over virtually all securities. The revisions made to the UCC have made that authority even more sweeping, since direct securities ownership has been eliminated for most individual and institutional investors.

Perhaps the most surprising fact to me about the DTC is that it is a member bank of the Federal Reserve System, with an account at the Federal Reserve Bank of New York. That status, along with its SIFMU designation, makes DTC subject to oversight from the Federal Reserve's board of governors.[94]

This means that the Federal Reserve's reach extends far beyond monetary policy. By regulating the centralized hub (i.e., DTC) through which virtually all stocks, bonds, and other securities are held, the Federal Reserve indirectly holds sway over the infrastructure of securities ownership. In this sense, the Federal Reserve is not only the world's most important monetary institution; it also exerts influence over more wealth than any other organization in the world. However, much of what the Federal Reserve does is shielded from public view.

Federal law prohibits the public and even government auditors from knowing much of what goes on inside the Federal Reserve. Mark Calabria, the chief statistician of the United States in the U.S. Office of Management and Budget and a former senior adviser at the Cato Institute, explained that while the Federal Reserve is subject to basic financial audits, four provisions in current law prevent the Government Accountability Office (GAO) from reviewing anything related to monetary policy.[95] He noted that these restrictions bar audits of "the deliberations of the Fed's monetary policy-setting body, the Federal Open Market Committee (FOMC), the communications of the FOMC to enact the policy decided upon, and the actual transactions conducted by the New York Federal Reserve to carry out the policy."[96]

In other words, the Federal Reserve's most important activities—deciding policy and executing it in financial markets—are off-limits to government auditors. When these restrictions were first adopted in the 1970s, GAO warned Congress,

> We do not see how we can satisfactorily audit the Federal Reserve System without authority to examine the largest single category of financial transactions and assets that it has.[97]

This lack of transparency becomes particularly consequential in a crisis, when the Federal Reserve's role could extend well beyond monetary policy decisions.

Because DTC is a member bank of the Federal Reserve System, additional federal emergency powers could come into play. This is largely uncharted legal territory, and it is unlikely to be tested unless the nation faces a severe financial crisis. It is impossible to say for certain how courts would respond to legal challenges over the federal government's authority, but we should still ask questions.

One little-known statute illustrates how far those emergency powers could reach. Section 95 of Title 12 of the U.S. Code grants the president and the secretary of the Treasury authority over Federal

Reserve member banks whenever the president declares a national emergency. DTC is one of those banks.

According to Section 95, during an emergency, no member bank of the Federal Reserve System may conduct "any normal banking business" except as permitted by the Treasury Department, with the president's approval. The statute imposes criminal penalties of up to $10,000 and a ten-year prison sentence, with each day of violation constituting a separate offense.[98]

The wording of this statute is somewhat vague, so it is difficult to predict how it could be applied in the future, or how it might affect DTC and the securities it holds (assets valued in the tens of trillions of dollars). It is clear, however, that Section 95 applies to every member bank of the Federal Reserve System, and since DTC is one of those banks, the federal government could assert tremendous authority over its operations during an emergency.

Whether Section 95 or other emergency-powers laws are ever applied to DTC, the fact remains that the stocks and bonds in your retirement account and other securities you believe you own are not truly yours. They exist in a system that you do not control and, in a major financial collapse, could be taken from you if lawmakers or Wall Street decided it was necessary for system stability. Your savings and investments could vanish overnight due to laws you have likely never heard of.

That possibility alone is more than enough to make me think twice before placing most of my wealth in securities.

IS THERE NOTHING TO FEAR?

Supporters of the current system do have several arguments to assure the public that there's nothing to fear. Here are the three most common:

Objection 1: SIPC insurance will protect Americans.

The first defense in support of the system is that most consumers are protected by the Securities Investor Protection Corporation (SIPC). SIPC works much like the Federal Deposit Insurance Corporation (FDIC): FDIC covers bank deposits, while SIPC covers brokerage accounts. SIPC promises up to $500,000 in protection for securities and cash, with $250,000 being the maximum for cash alone.[99] Supporters insist that this level of coverage is more than enough for most Americans. They also argue that many large brokers carry private policies extending additional coverage to their client investors.[100]

However, that doesn't exactly mean that there's nothing to worry about. SIPC is (and has long been) substantially underfunded. At the end of 2024, its reserve fund totaled less than $5 billion, a tiny fraction of the securities held by U.S. brokers and banks.[101] Fidelity alone administers more than $16 trillion in assets,[102] meaning that only 0.03 percent of those assets would be covered by SIPC. And, though Fidelity provides private "excess of SIPC" insurance to its customers, this provides only an extra $1 billion in aggregate coverage[103]—a negligible amount compared to Fidelity's total size. In the event of a true systemic collapse, both SIPC and private excess insurance would be quickly exhausted.

The truth is, no institution has anything close to the resources needed to bail out even a small percentage of the market. These safety nets were designed to handle the failure of a handful of firms. They are not designed to handle the implosion of Wall Street itself.

Objection 2: Wall Street is safe and stable.

A second argument is that Wall Street and the financial system are generally healthy, and that a systemic crash is therefore unlikely. There are, however, many good reasons to doubt that assumption.

Americans have been told that before—and have then watched as markets collapsed. On the eve of the Great Recession in late 2007, most of Wall Street had no idea how fragile the system had become. By the time the stock market plunged in 2008 and ordinary Americans realized a crisis was underway, it was already too late.

Markets may appear stable today, but there is no guarantee that the appearance of stability will continue. The structural problems described earlier remain unresolved and will continue unresolved until large-scale reforms are made. The question is not whether Wall Street seems stable right now but whether you believe it will remain stable permanently. To restore investor control and property rights, reform is essential.

Objection 3: Centralization is a great benefit.

A third objection is that eliminating direct, registered securities ownership has been a positive development. The old paper-certificate system, through which investors retained stronger property rights, was bogged down by paperwork, long wait times, and growing complexity. By centralizing ownership and digitizing markets, transactions became faster, cheaper, and easier to manage.

There is no denying that today's system is more efficient and accessible. Centralization has made investing more affordable and attractive, boosting participation by individuals, businesses, pensions, investment firms, and banks alike. But the price of those efficiencies has been the erosion of property rights and, with them, financial security in the event of a crash.

That trade-off, however, was neither necessary nor inevitable. The markets could have been modernized without stripping investors of ownership. American and English property law has long recognized arrangements (bailment agreements, for example) allowing one party to hold property for another while preserving ownership rights.[104]

This raises the question: If efficiency didn't require destroying those rights, why did lawmakers and Wall Street insist on doing so?

I believe one benefit is easy to see if we consider the question from Wall Street's perspective. Centralization gave institutions control, making every aspect of securities trading cheaper and more convenient. They could seize full ownership without resistance, so why wouldn't they?

Centralizing control of securities triggered massive growth in Wall Street activity and profits. In the 1950s, the New York Stock Exchange (NYSE) had an average daily trading volume of approximately a million shares or less.[105] By 1970, just before DTC's launch, daily volume had climbed to 12 million shares.[106] After DTC's creation and the first round of Uniform Commercial Code amendments making the new system possible, trading skyrocketed. By 1990, average daily volume reached 157 million shares, an increase of more than 1,200 percent in just two decades.

In the 1990s, when the UCC was revised again, the changes codified the security entitlement concept, eliminated direct property rights to securities, and handed too-big-to-fail banks priority over investors' assets in certain insolvency cases, as described earlier.

By 1995, daily trading volume had climbed to 346 million shares. It surpassed 1 billion just five years later, and by the onset of the Great Recession in late 2007, it had reached 3.17 billion.[107] Today, in 2025, the NYSE alone often exceeds 5 billion shares a day, while Nasdaq regularly tops 8 billion.[108]

Remember: in 1970, NYSE volume was only about 12 million shares per day. Daily trading has exploded by billions of shares since DTC's creation and the related UCC changes and is now more than four hundred times what it was in 1970. Each additional trade translates into more fees for broker-dealers and more profits for the banks and financial firms behind them.

Here's an illustration of how much Wall Street profits have

ballooned since DTC's creation. In 1970, Merrill Lynch reported net income of $40.7 million,[109] equivalent to about $338 million in today's dollars.[110] The firm is now the centerpiece of Bank of America's wealth management division, which earned a profit of $4.3 billion in 2024.[111] That means that its most recently reported income is more than a hundred times greater than it was in 1970 in nominal terms, and is roughly thirteen times greater after adjusting for inflation. The comparison may not be perfect, but the point is clear: profits under the DTC system have soared.

Another benefit Wall Street gained from the DTC model is stock lending. Centralized ownership made it easy for large institutions to lend securities to other investors, often for short selling. Short selling occurs when investors bet a stock or asset will lose value, allowing them to profit from its decline. It's essentially a wager that a company or market is overvalued or headed for trouble.

In an interview with the SEC Historical Society, former DTC chairman and CEO Bill Jaenike admitted that stock lending had increased dramatically because of DTC. He was asked whether the creation of DTC and the shift to the book-entry system had impacted trading patterns.[112]

Jaenike pointed to two key areas that benefited the most. The first was trade volume. In the 1960s and early 1970s, Wall Street could never have handled billions of daily trades, as mentioned earlier. The second, Jaenike said, was "the stock loan business, which has grown exponentially over the years." As he put it, "The trading that you see now could not possibly have been done with physical certificates."[113]

Derivatives markets have increased dramatically with this new system. As I noted in chapter 1, a derivative is a financial contract whose value depends on—or is derived from—the price of something else, such as a stock, bond, commodity, interest rate, or even another derivative. Common examples include options, futures, and swaps. A derivative is basically a bet on the future price of something.

Derivatives can be used to hedge risk, speculate on price movements, or magnify gains and losses. They are powerful tools but can also be very risky, especially when heavily leveraged. In practice, many investors use them to gamble on markets.

The DTC model centralized custody of securities in electronic form, replacing physical certificates. That shift made buying, selling, and transferring securities vastly more efficient, reliable, and scalable—conditions that led to the modern derivatives market, where underlying assets change hands constantly and contracts are repriced daily.

The derivatives market is staggering in scale, so much so that it can be difficult to comprehend. It's often estimated that the global derivatives market is as high as $1 quadrillion. "How can that be?" asked writer J. B. Maverick in a 2024 article. "Largely because there are numerous derivatives in existence, available on virtually every possible type of investment asset, including equities, commodities, bonds, and currency. Some market analysts even place the size of the market at more than 10 times that of the total world gross domestic product (GDP)."[114]

Meanwhile, Wall Street firms earn billions each year from derivatives trading—profits that would be only a fraction as large without the centralized, security entitlement–based system created by DTC and Article 8.

I want to stop here for a moment and state that I'm a proud capitalist. I believe in creating value and rewarding success. But I must also state the reality: Wall Street's richest institutions have grown even wealthier largely because they removed ordinary investors' ability to directly own the securities they paid for and thought they owned. At best, that trade-off is unfair; at worst, it is deeply immoral. The institutions that engineered this system and the lawmakers who enabled it *should* guarantee that if Wall Street goes belly-up, investors get their assets back before anything goes to bailing out the too-big-to-fail banks.

There's little question as to Wall Street's motivation to create the Depository Trust Company: the system was tailor-made to consolidate power and profits. The bigger question is, in my mind, why did lawmakers go along? The Uniform Commercial Code isn't federal law; it has to be enacted state by state. Why did every state legislature agree to reduce property rights for their constituents? Why did the states give banks legal priority over investors whenever their securities are pledged as collateral?

Voters didn't ask for this. Businesses and investment firms outside the Wall Street cartel didn't want it either. State lawmakers had no direct financial incentive. What was it that made them willing to impose such radical changes to the Uniform Commercial Code?

HOW WE GOT HERE

The truth is, most lawmakers who passed the revisions to the UCC stripping investors of meaningful property rights to their assets didn't know what they were doing. As noted previously in this chapter, the UCC is extremely complicated. Because of this complexity, lawmakers primarily rely on two organizations to help them make changes to the UCC: the Uniform Law Commission (ULC) and, more indirectly, the American Law Institute (ALI).

As their names would suggest, the ULC and ALI are composed primarily of law professors and practicing lawyers. Together, these two organizations govern the entirety of the UCC and regularly develop model legislation meant to change it.[115] When the ULC and ALI make suggestions, state lawmakers almost always listen.

In fairness, it's unrealistic to expect state legislators to master every complex bill that comes before them. Unlike members of Congress, most state legislators don't have large staffs (and in some cases, no staff at all) to research and explain the details. When a highly technical UCC bill comes before them, endorsed by legislative leaders and backed by the ULC or ALI, they typically go along with it. After all, legislators cannot become commercial law experts overnight.

In many cases, lawmakers are only as good as the information they receive. In the case of the UCC, policymakers have been led to believe that they can trust the drafters and their advocates, with no questions asked.

The reason for that trust stems from the reputation of the ULC and ALI as nonpartisan experts in their fields, whose only goal is to help lawmakers create policy benefiting society. That reputation, however, is a complete façade.

In practice, these two organizations have repeatedly promoted policies that expand the centralized power held by ruling-class elites, government officials, large financial institutions, and other special interests, and, at the same time, diminish the rights of individuals. Their track record in recent years shows a pattern of opposing reforms that would protect or restore those rights, including efforts by some state lawmakers to address the very problems described throughout this chapter.

The ULC and ALI are best known for controlling the UCC, but their reach extends far beyond commercial law. A look at who has been running these organizations in recent years will make it clear why their recommendations are so often skewed toward increasing the power of the few.[116,117]

One prime example is Richard Revesz, who directed ALI from 2014 to 2023 and helped shape many of its major initiatives.[118] After leaving ALI, President Joe Biden appointed him head of the Office of Information and Regulatory Affairs,[119] a position often called the "rules czar." [120] In that role, Revesz wielded considerable influence over federal regulations, government data collection, statistical standards, and privacy policies.[121] Many of the rules advanced under his watch, particularly in the realm of climate and environmental policy, represented significant expansions of federal control over the economy and private industry and led Bloomberg Law to label him "the most progressive rules czar."[122]

After Revesz's departure, ALI selected former federal appellate judge Diane P. Wood as his successor.[123,124] Wood, who served as chief judge of the Seventh Circuit from 2013 to 2020,[125] has a long record of upholding expansive government authority. Her decisions, including supporting Illinois's strict COVID-19 lockdowns and rejecting challenges to certain firearms restrictions,[126,127] reflected the same institutional mindset that has long guided ALI and the ULC: a preference for centralizing power, especially in times of crisis.

In addition to leaders such as Revesz and Wood, ALI's advisory ranks have also included figures like Janet Napolitano. Napolitano served as U.S. secretary of Homeland Security under President Barack Obama, was an influential member of President Joe Biden's Intelligence Advisory Board,[128] and is a "life member" of the ALI's Council.[129,130] Her career has consistently placed her at the center of expansive federal security and surveillance powers, the same orientation that mirrors ALI and the ULC's broader philosophy of centralized authority.

This philosophy is not limited to the individuals who lead or advise these organizations. Official organizational policies reflect it, too. In 2023, the ULC advanced one of its most revealing proposals yet: the Public-Health Emergency Authority Act (PHEAA).[131] This model legislation would give state governors far-reaching, open-ended powers during declared public health emergencies.[132]

Under the PHEAA, governors could declare health emergencies, impose sweeping regulations statewide, and renew their powers indefinitely with minimal oversight. They would have authority over virtually every aspect of life, including the "zoning, operation, commandeering, management, or use" of buildings, parks, outdoor areas, and other facilities; the "testing, isolation, quarantine, movement, gathering, evacuation, or relocation" of individuals; and the "acquisition, allocation, distribution, management, or spending" of public funds. The bill also grants control over the destruction or relocation of animals and plants, as well as broad surveillance and monitoring powers tied to public health "or any of its effects."[133]

Even more concerning, the PHEAA would allow governors to unilaterally suspend existing laws, orders, or regulations they deemed obstructive, effectively allowing them to override state statutes at will. Although emergency orders would nominally expire within forty-five to ninety days, the bill allows unlimited renewals with only minimal procedural steps and no requirement for legislative approval. Legislatures must be notified and given an "opportunity" to convene, but their consent is not necessary.[134]

That the ULC not only endorsed but drafted such legislation underscores its willingness to concentrate extraordinary, discretionary power in the executive branch. This same mindset extends into its work on the Uniform Commercial Code.

Though initiatives such as the PHEAA are highly concerning in their own right, the Uniform Commercial Code has been the ULC and ALI's most powerful vehicle for rewriting the legal foundations of society, often in ways that benefit monolithic financial institutions at the expense of individual liberty. Beyond the already-discussed Article 8 changes that removed your property rights to your own financial assets, these organizations have recently advanced amendments to other UCC articles that lay the legal groundwork for a central bank digital currency (CBDC) and the tokenization of real-world assets,[135] both of which carry profound implications for personal freedom and property rights. (In a later chapter, I will go into more detail about CBDCs, such as the unique, totalitarian threats they pose and how they could be deployed in a future financial crisis.)

Though discussing them in detail is outside the scope of this chapter, these proposed amendments could strip away even more property rights and greatly reduce individual liberties. The ULC, ALI, and powerful financial institutions already gutted your property rights to securities decades ago, but that wasn't enough. Now, they are working to extend that model by facilitating centralized control over your bank deposits—and, potentially, nearly all your physical assets.[136]

The ULC and ALI introduced the new UCC amendments—which revise Article 9 and establish a new Article 12—and recommended them for adoption in 2022. However, as of August 2025, thirty-one states and the District of Columbia have already adopted these changes, including major "red states" such as Florida and "blue states" such as California and Illinois.[137]

The rapid and widespread embrace of these amendments mirrors how the Article 8 revisions were quietly adopted decades earlier. Clearly, lawmakers still widely regard the ULC and ALI as credible and trustworthy sources of legal guidance. This is astounding to me, considering their track record of promoting policies that erode personal freedom, attack property rights, empower government control over citizens' lives, and serve inordinately powerful special financial interests. I want to ask how lawmakers can trust or continue to accept guidance from people like that on anything.

The pattern is clear. The ULC and ALI have consistently advanced proposals—through the UCC, the PHEAA, and other model laws—that shift power and wealth away from individuals and toward centralized authorities. These efforts move quietly through state legislatures with little public debate or understanding of their consequences and are shielded from scrutiny by their drafters' reputations and the technical complexity of their work. Until lawmakers and the public recognize the stakes, these seemingly obscure changes will continue to erode core freedoms under the guise of legal modernization.

THE CAMPAIGN FOR DTC

In the 1970s, industry lobbyists and the Uniform Law Commission pressed state legislatures to adopt changes to the Uniform Commercial Code that would remove legal barriers to the Depository Trust Company's centralized, book-entry system. Though DTC launched in 1973, many state laws still required physical certificates and direct registration, making full use of a centralized depository difficult, if not impossible.[138]

As noted earlier in this chapter, UCC Article 8 had to be revised to accommodate this new structure. And it was. Throughout the late 1970s and early 1980s, every state adopted these amendments, bringing their laws into alignment with the centralized DTC model.[139] These changes marked the first major revisions to Article 8. The second round of revisions in the 1990s went much further, changing the fundamental definition of what it means to "own" a security.

We don't know exactly what lawmakers were told about the implications of centralizing securities ownership, but we do have a glimpse of how the changes were presented and sold to lawmakers.

In a 2011 interview with the SEC Historical Society, William Dentzer, the first chairman and CEO of DTC (and a central figure in its creation), explained how Wall Street lobbyists worked with the ULC to push revisions through state legislatures. Dentzer's account offers rare insight into how lawmakers were persuaded to cede direct ownership of securities in favor of a centralized system.[140]

"We worked with the relevant committees of the different state legislatures, and persuaded them that adopting this model, the Uniform Code amendment, was the right thing to do," Dentzer said during the interview. "Other states were doing it. Why don't they get with it? They're going to penalize their financial institutions if they didn't do the same thing."[141]

I have had a lot of experience in legislative battles involving the Uniform Law Commission, and I can tell you that is exactly how the ULC still operates today. "Everyone else is doing it," they say. "And if you don't do it, too, then your state is going to face dire economic consequences."

Many lawmakers don't understand the intricacies of commercial law, so they listen. They are often afraid of getting things horribly wrong. So they "get with it," just as Dentzer said.

Dentzer further explained that, once the largest states signed on, the remainder became far easier to sway: "[Once] the major states had enacted the necessary laws, our lawyers felt that if any questions arose, we would prevail, and our participants would prevail. So we decided we had enough states on board to go ahead."[142]

This is another tactic frequently used by the Uniform Law Commission and its allies. Once several of the larger states (such as California, New York, and Texas) adopt legislation, it becomes much harder for smaller states to resist. The Uniform Commercial Code is supposed to be "uniform" across all the states, so holdout states and their lawmakers are villainized until they, too, give in. The same playbook was used throughout the 1990s and early 2000s, when the second round of Article 8 revisions was rolled out and eventually adopted by every state. These tactics are still deployed today, as the ULC and banking industry lobbyists pressure holdout states into adopting other concerning UCC amendments.

That, then, is the answer to the question of why so many state lawmakers agreed to reduce your ownership rights to securities. Bank lobbyists and ethically compromised lawyers convinced them that the changes were not only harmless but a strong improvement to commercial law—and warned of the chaos and blame lawmakers would face if they refused the amendments.

No one wants to be blamed for causing financial turmoil or preventing economic growth. That's what lawmakers were told would

happen if they didn't comply with the demands of so-called "experts."
Once some states started to adopt the new rules, others went along
for the ride.

UNCOVERING THE TRUTH

Over the course of this chapter, I've traced how a series of deliberate
legal changes reshaped the very nature of securities ownership in
America, and shown that these changes were pushed by the banking
industry and its allies in the Uniform Law Commission. I examined
how revisions to UCC Article 8 removed direct property rights, how
secured creditors gained priority over investors' own assets, and how
supposed consumer protections collapse under stress. I also presented
crisis scenarios, from broker insolvency to sweeping emergency
powers, where these vulnerabilities could be exploited.

This system now depends on three things: the loss of direct
ownership, the subordination of investors to "systemically important"
financial institutions, and the erosion of safeguards that once put
ordinary investors first. In this system, "ownership" is largely nominal.
In the wrong set of circumstances, your assets could be taken by
others, and you would have no legal recourse.

It might appear that the effort to take genuine ownership rights
away from investors and hand control to a small circle of powerful
interests was only the work of large financial institutions and Wall
Street firms. It might seem that the Uniform Law Commission and
American Law Institute acted as crucial accomplices, persuading
lawmakers to pass the Uniform Commercial Code revisions that
enabled this shift. The truth actually goes a bit deeper.

The individuals who played the decisive roles in this overhaul
of the system were powerful and well-connected. Their influence
extended beyond Wall Street and the legal profession, into realms of

wealth and national security that rarely come under public scrutiny.

I still have many questions about this topic, but years of investigation suggest that this campaign may have originated with one of the world's wealthiest families, working with a former CIA operative to transform Wall Street and consolidate control on an unprecedented scale. These connections—and the evidence supporting them—are the focus of the next chapter. There we will examine who these figures were, how they shaped the system we have today, and why their influence still matters.

In later chapters, we'll turn to what can be done about it, because while the vulnerabilities in this system are real and deeply entrenched, they are not insurmountable.

3

THE TRUTH ABOUT DTC'S ORIGINS: THE MEN BEHIND HISTORY'S GREATEST PROPERTY RIGHTS HEIST

Revolutions are not always marked by battlefields or political coups. Some happen quietly in boardrooms, where decisions are made with no votes or headlines yet reshape the lives of millions.

As I explained in chapter 2, a revolution took place in the financial world during the latter half of the twentieth century. It changed the meaning of property ownership in America, took away the direct legal claim of ordinary citizens to most securities investments, and concentrated (unprecedented) power in the hands of a small, little-known institution: the Depository Trust Company (DTC). Some might call it one of the greatest heists in history.

To be clear, no one's property was *legally* stolen. It was a plan that led people into giving their direct ownership rights away, and many did not realize they had done so. As a result, most Americans now face great risks that did not exist previously. People still have a significant amount of control over their securities investments, but true, registered ownership of securities is largely a thing of the past.

This change happened under William Dentzer, a leader who could win the confidence of powerful institutions, navigate political realities, and bring together competing interests behind a single vision. For many Americans, that name means nothing; yet his actions helped set the stage for the system in which a single entity controls tens of trillions of dollars. Dentzer had an unusual career path. He was not a Wall Street prodigy or a lifelong banker. He moved through important but little-understood positions in government and student activism. He then became the founding head of DTC, one of the most important financial organizations in modern history.

I see Dentzer's story as a lens through which to examine the much larger drama of the past one hundred years, with powerful political figures, bankers, and global operators. The story of Dentzer's unlikely rise is also the story of the networks of influence, institutional ambitions, and personal alliances that converged to create DTC and remake the rules of ownership.

Deliberate choices and nontransparent motives led to the financial transformation that shapes the markets today. Understanding those origins brings out an unsettling truth: the loss of the individual's direct ownership over investments was not an unavoidable consequence of modernization; it was carried out by people who knew what they were doing.

If the day comes when a financial crash wipes out some or many of America's large broker-deals and banks, the fact that you do not directly own the stocks, bonds, and other securities that you invested in could mean financial ruin for you and millions of others. You could be affected even if you don't have any securities investments: the entire economy will likely collapse under such circumstances, as more individuals and institutions come to distrust the DTC model.[143]

In this chapter, we will investigate the incredible theories that could explain why those changes were made and who the major players were that caused them.

Keep in mind that there is still much that we do *not* know, and even more that we will likely never understand. I will provide you with most of the known facts about DTC and its origins, and I will offer best guesses about potential causes and the motivations of key players in the institutions that helped to create DTC. I will try to make it clear when I am discussing well-documented history and when I am speculating. I urge you to do your own homework, starting with the sources given in the endnotes.

THE MAN

By nearly all accounts, William Dentzer was a patriotic, highly successful Wall Street innovator. He was the head of the Depository Trust Company for two decades. Dentzer helped to transform the global securities market. He cured the securities paperwork crisis that affected broker-dealers and other financial institutions in the 1960s. As a result, costs associated with buying and selling securities dropped dramatically, exchanges became more accessible than ever, and many middle-class Americans began investing for the first time. Trading volumes on the New York Stock Exchange and other securities exchanges soared. The modern stock market exists in large part due to William Dentzer.[144]

Dentzer appears to have been beloved by his family and

community. Dentzer and his wife were married for sixty-eight years. Bill Dentzer's daughter, Susan Dentzer, a successful businessperson in her own right, called him the "greatest father from a great generation."[145] Bill Dentzer was a loving husband, father, and grandfather. He also served his community: in a leadership position in a local Presbyterian church, on the board of his local public library, and on the board of trustees for Muskingum University, Dentzer's alma mater.[146]

But there was more to Dentzer than what appeared on the surface. Prior to his time at DTC, Dentzer lived a life full of secrets, some of which might help to explain how the modern securities market was made and others which might help us understand why property rights were eliminated, or at least why it was Dentzer who led the effort.[147]

THE PLOT

Who were the most important people and institutions behind the creation of the DTC model? Who led the charge to reduce your property rights? And most important of all, why did they do it? Those three questions have bothered me: although there are many sources that describe the official story behind why the DTC was created (that Wall Street's "paperwork crisis" needed to be solved), certain aspects of the established narrative do not make sense.

I'll start with the official account of DTC's creation. The following is a small part of a lengthy history of the DTC, published by a historical office affiliated with the Securities and Exchange Commission (SEC). According to the report,

For the securities industry, the 1960s was a decade that began with great promise but ended in crisis. As the decade began, the securities industry was enjoying the prosperity of an economic resurgence. Capital needs of American business were growing, public participation in the market was increasing, and institutional trading was becoming a major force in the stock market. Average daily trade volume on the NYSE reflected this, growing from 3 million shares per day in 1960 to 12 million in 1970.

Concurrent with the growth in trade volume came an increase in the pressure on brokers' back offices. Transaction processing—always labor intensive—became a serious threat to market efficiency as the decade progressed. On April 1, 1968, trading on the NYSE broke the previous record of October 29, 1929, nearly four decades earlier. Before the year ended, the record was broken an additional 24 times and the expression "paperwork crisis" had entered the nation's lexicon.[148]

According to the SEC Historical Society, Wall Street had known for a long time that banks and investment broker-dealers would need a long-term resolution to the growing paperwork problem. The favored solution for many of the biggest institutions was the centralization of the control of securities. Instead of physically moving stock certificates, buying and selling certificates could be accomplished using a "book-entry" system. All the securities could be held in one place, and then large institutions would assign and reassign securities on paper. This is essentially the strategy that led to DTC in the 1970s.

Throughout the 1960s, there were several large institutions that laid the foundation for this new way of buying, selling, and holding securities, beginning with a pilot program launched in 1961. The SEC Historical Society notes,

In mid-1961, the [New York Stock Exchange], together with Bankers Trust Company, the Chase Manhattan Bank, NA, and First National City Bank of New York initiated the 'Pilot Operation for Central Handling of Securities.'

Beginning with 15 securities and 31 firms, deliveries were made between members by book-entry and without the physical movement of certificates. Over the course of the pilot, which ended in early 1962, 14 million shares were delivered, demonstrating book-entry delivery's practicality.[149]

Chase Manhattan Bank (later JPMorganChase) was a key institution behind the pilot program. (Chase Bank and its leadership will play a pivotal role in other parts of this story.)

Once the New York Stock Exchange and the other institutions decided that a book-entry system could solve the paperwork crisis, they set out to have state laws changed so that such a model was legal. At that time, the Uniform Commercial Code (discussed at length in the previous chapter) included legal provisions that would have made a book-entry model impossible.

In its history of DTC, the SEC Historical Society explains,

Before a certificate processing and safekeeping service could be initiated, it was necessary to secure amendments to Article 8 of the Uniform Commercial Code (UCC) that would sanction the transfer of ownership or pledge of securities by depository book-entry in lieu of delivering physical certificates. That effort began in 1962, and the last state's amendment was obtained in 1970. However, by the mid-1960s, enough states had passed enabling legislation to encourage the New York Stock Exchange, together with a core of New York Clearing House (NYCH) banks, to proceed to work out the details of the proposed service.

Plans called for immobilizing in a vault the millions of certificates held in "street name" by NYSE member firms. Transfer of ownership among members could then be accomplished with accounting entries—"book-entry"—eliminating physical certificate movement and the mushrooming paperwork needed to transfer them.[150]

The New York Stock Exchange launched the Central Certificate Service (CCS) in 1968, and by the end of 1969, "[broker-dealers] had 464 million shares on deposit with CCS."[151] The CCS, however, worked only within the New York Stock Exchange, and it didn't allow for many interindustry interactions, which was a huge issue due to institutional trading skyrocketing.[152] Congress and federal regulatory agencies were demanding further reforms to reduce costs and increase efficiency.[153]

Large banks (who at the time held significant amounts of the country's securities investments) joined together with several large securities institutions to create a new organization called the Banking and Securities Industry Committee (BASIC). BASIC was led by JPMorgan's chairman and CEO, John Meyer Jr.; the executive director was Herman Bevis, a retired partner at Price Waterhouse, one of the country's most important accounting and auditing firms.[154]

The SEC Historical Society records,

Throughout 1970 and much of 1971, BASIC acted on 14 projects designed to reduce the costs and improve the process of securities operations. The most significant of these was the establishment of a Comprehensive Securities Depository System (CSDS) expanding upon the NYSE's Central Certificate Service. In September of 1971, BASIC announced the signing of a Memorandum of Understanding among the New York and American Stock Exchanges, the National Association of Securities Dealers, and the eleven member banks of the New York Clearing House Association, toward this end. Regional markets and banks soon joined in the process and a National Coordinating Group (NCG) was formed.[155]

BASIC and the interests it represented embraced the idea of building a national, interindustry depository to hold most, if not all, of the country's securities. Someone was needed to lead this effort to centralize the nation's investments, be responsible for convincing the country's financial institutions that this new project was essential, and get everyone on board. This is where William Dentzer enters our story.

In an interview with the SEC Historical Society, Dentzer explained that, in 1972, BASIC leaders Meyer and Bevis asked him to run their new depository (which later was named DTC). According to Dentzer's account of the offer, "They wanted, as a culmination of their work, to create a securities depository chartered as a trust company in New York which could hold securities for similar to-be-formed trust companies in other states."[156]

At the time BASIC recruited Dentzer, he was serving as the New York superintendent of banks, the chief regulator of banks in the state.[157] During that period, the New York superintendent of banks was one of the most important regulatory positions in the country because many of the largest banks were state chartered, which meant state regulatory agencies had greater power over banking than they do today, and many of the largest banks in the country were headquartered in New York.

At this point in the story, the creation of DTC and the reimagining of how people own securities seems rather straightforward. Banks and broker-dealers had a paperwork crisis to solve. The best way to do it seemed to be centralizing the control and eventually the ownership of investment securities. Banks and other major players on Wall Street created BASIC to put all of the pieces into place. BASIC hired William Dentzer, the head New York bank regulator, to lead the effort, an apparently logical choice since banks were closely involved in the creation of DTC.

However, as I started to investigate how this new system began, I noticed two things immediately. First (as discussed in the previous chapter), industry leaders could have designed the DTC model so that individuals retained full ownership rights of the securities. There was no need to reduce property rights to solve the paperwork crisis. I wondered why they had chosen to do it that way. At least one reason (covered in detail in chapter 2) is that financial institutions realized they could make more money if they controlled one institution that had direct, registered ownership of securities. (It helped create the modern derivatives market, for example, which has yielded a tremendous amount of wealth for broker-dealers in recent years.)

The second thing that raised serious concerns for me was that Dentzer seemed completely unqualified to lead DTC. He had been in the head bank regulator position in New York only since 1970, just a few years before BASIC recruited him.[158] Prior to being named the New York superintendent of banks, Dentzer had no experience either in banking or on Wall Street.

Dentzer himself said that the only reason he got the job of regulating New York's banks was because another (more qualified) person wanted Dentzer to save the position for him while he worked on Nelson Rockefeller's gubernatorial reelection campaign.[159] (Rockefeller was a powerful Republican in the 1960s and 70s. He became governor of New York in 1959 and later went on to become vice president to Gerald Ford, after President Richard Nixon resigned in the wake of the Watergate scandal.)

Dentzer was chosen to be the chief bank regulator of New York, America's banking capital and the most important financial center in the world, because of a need to "save the seat" for someone else. In his interview with the SEC Historical Society in 2011, Dentzer described the unusual turn of events:

Frank Wille, who was the Superintendent of Banks at the time, was named to be head of the FDIC. Someone needed to take his place. The governor's deputy secretary, Harry Albright, wanted to be the Superintendent, but Governor Rockefeller, especially looking forward to another run as governor, didn't want to let Harry go. I had gotten to know Harry because he was the Governor's Appointment Secretary.

So, in my coming to New York, establishing the council, and clearing arrangements for our work through him, we'd gotten to know each other well. And Harry came to me at one point and said, "Would you like to be Superintendent of Banks for a while? It's a job that I would like to get at some point, but the Governor won't let me go." I said, "Yes."[160]

As Dentzer explains in the quote above, when he was chosen to be the top New York bank regulator, he was working for a New York economic policy council. He's referring to the New York Council of Economic Advisers, which was established by Nelson Rockefeller to help spur economic development in the state.[161] Rockefeller chose Eugene Black, a former president of the World Bank and an influential figure in his own right, to run the council, and in 1969, Black chose Dentzer to be the council's executive director.[162]

That was the year that Dentzer moved to New York for the first time.[163] He had, according to my research, no domestic policy experience, no experience running a business, little to no experience managing domestic economic issues, and little to no banking experience. One year later, Dentzer was appointed to be superintendent of banks, one of the most important bank regulators in America. Two years after that, Dentzer was put in charge of what would become DTC, which would house more wealth than any other nongovernment institution in the world. This was all without any well-connected family members, without marrying into one of America's elite families, and without any experience working on Wall Street.[164]

Dentzer's story is one of the most unexpected rises to power I have ever heard (and I have heard many during my career in public policy). Dentzer's lack of experience and expertise raised a very large red flag in my research. Why was Dentzer chosen for so many vital roles in government and business? What did men like Eugene Black, Nelson Rockefeller, and the leaders of the top banks in New York see in him? Surely these men had known someone on Wall Street or in banking more qualified to take over the DTC project than Dentzer.

I realized that if I wanted to fully understand why DTC came to exist, I needed to understand who William Dentzer was. The official story of DTC didn't seem quite right to me. What I learned as I researched this shocked me (and I am not easily shocked).

WHO WAS THE REAL WILLIAM DENTZER?

In 1929, William Dentzer was born in Rochester, Pennsylvania, which he described as a "bedroom community for steel mill workers in the Pittsburgh area."[165] Dentzer wrote of his high school experience: "I was an honor student, class president in my junior and senior years, co-editor of the school newspaper, and a football player."[166] He earned a scholarship to attend the University of Pittsburgh, but, in 1947, he ended up enrolling in Muskingum University instead. Muskingum is a private university in New Concord, Ohio, located about two hours west of Pittsburgh.

Dentzer excelled at Muskingum. He was a member of the college football team and was heavily involved in the school's debate team. In fact, he and his debate partner ended up winning an Ohio college debate team championship. His fellow students elected him class president in his sophomore and junior years and student body president in his senior year.

In 1948, while still a student at Muskingum, Dentzer began

his involvement in the National Student Association (NSA), an organization that would alter the trajectory of his life. He served as a delegate to the NSA's Congress and, in 1951, joined the organization's National Executive Committee. When elected NSA president, Dentzer adopted his predecessor's goal of "creating a free-world alternative to the [c]ommunist front International Union of Students (IUS)."[167]

NSA was a remarkably successful student organization at the time Dentzer became its president. Dentzer described NSA as "then the most representative student organization in America." Its ideological views were driven by a fervent opposition to communism, but it also promoted a more traditional form of American progressivism as well. According to Dentzer, "it stood for responsible student engagement on campus, opposition to racial discrimination and McCarthyism, expressing student views on national issues affecting higher education, and advancing international efforts to support student freedom and welfare in other countries."[168]

By 1953, Dentzer had graduated from college and was working for the NSA. Part of his responsibilities involved traveling across the country to gain support for the organization. The same year, he was a representative for the first International Student Conference (ISC), which took place in Scotland. The ISC existed largely as a direct opponent to communist student groups in Europe and elsewhere.[169]

NSA had a relatively small budget. Dentzer said, "I spent most of my year traveling to meet with student governments across the country, frequently sleeping on couches or dormitory floors along the way."[170] However, a significant amount of the money the organization received came from the CIA.[171]

Accounts differ about exactly how and when the CIA started funding the National Student Association, as well as who initiated the agreement. In an article authored by Dentzer, he noted that "to reduce criticism of the Agency, CIA Director Richard Helms told *The New York Times* that its support was in response to my request as

NSA president. While this was untrue, it was irrelevant to everyone but me."[172]

Other sources, however, claim that Dentzer knew about the CIA funding earlier than he stated publicly, or, at the very least, that he knew that not-well-known figures in government were behind a significant amount of the NSA's funding.[173]

Regardless of whether Dentzer sparked the CIA's interest in the NSA, Dentzer was certainly aware of the CIA's involvement before the public learned about it. According to Dentzer's own account,

> Following my presidential year [in the NSA], Celia and I moved to the Netherlands, where I helped establish the [International Student Conference's] new Secretariat. Just prior to my departure for that post in the Netherlands and after signing a secrecy agreement, I was informed by a CIA officer that the money I had raised from a foundation to support NSA's international program had been covertly supplied by [the] CIA. I was told also that the CIA was prepared to provide covert support for future international programs of [the] NSA and the International Student Conference.[174]

Dentzer apparently had no problem with the CIA's support for the NSA. When the CIA's involvement eventually became widely known, in 1967 (much later in Dentzer's career), he publicly downplayed the NSA's decision to accept the funding. (It is important to note that this occurred at a time when the CIA was heavily criticized for its relationship with the popular student organization, since the CIA is supposed to limit its operations to foreign activities, not involve itself in domestic propaganda campaigns.) Dentzer stood by the NSA and CIA throughout the firestorm.[175] At the time the CIA's involvement with the NSA became public, few understood how far the CIA's reach had extended.

Dentzer spent a year in Europe helping to develop an international anti-communist student organization. He then enrolled in law school, first at Yale and then at the University of Pennsylvania.[176] However, the Army drafted him before he could finish his degree. He finished basic training and then, in 1956, the CIA recruited him.[177]

There is little information available about Dentzer's time in the CIA: I could find nothing in the public record about his role in the CIA, why he was recruited, or whether he was involved in any covert activities. To my knowledge, Dentzer never publicly discussed the responsibilities he had in the CIA. The many news articles about Dentzer over the years often mentioned that he served in the CIA but did not report any details about his service.

However, although there seem to be no firsthand accounts of Dentzer's CIA stint, at least two strong pieces of evidence suggest that he was engaged in secret government programs.

The first comes from Karen Paget, who conducted extensive research for her book *Patriotic Betrayal* (published by Yale University Press in 2015).[178] Paget holds a doctorate from the University of Colorado and has spent many years working in academia and in Washington, D.C., where she served in the Carter administration.[179] Her ideological views seem to fall, at least in my opinion, on the left side of the political spectrum; yet she has serious concerns about the CIA and its history, as do I.

Patriotic Betrayal focuses on the CIA's involvement in the National Student Association in the 1950s and 1960s. According to Paget's research, Dentzer played an important role that lasted long after he left the NSA. Dentzer is referenced more than one hundred times in *Patriotic Betrayal*; Paget includes countless quotes from key figures in the scandal, including Dentzer.[180]

Patriotic Betrayal records an interesting story that sheds some light on Dentzer's role in the CIA. In 1959, there was a meeting between Donald Hoffman, the NSA president at that time, and two

CIA operatives.[181]

According to Paget,

> Soon after Hoffman's election [in 1959], former NSA president Bob Kiley summoned him to Washington. After he arrived, [William] Dentzer joined them to discuss how the NSA was able to carry out its various programs and projects. Hoffman said later, "I had tremendous respect for Bob Kiley and had heard great things about Dentzer." When they assured him that all the previous officers had cooperated with the CIA, he signed the security oath. . . . Hoffman developed an affinity for CIA work, and continued his intelligence career for the next seven years.[182]

This meeting occurred in 1959, which was during the time that Dentzer was in the CIA. According to Denzter's own account, he joined the agency in 1956 and didn't leave until after President John F. Kennedy's election in 1960.[183] That means that while Dentzer was in the CIA, he was still involved in activities related to the National Student Association. (The CIA's involvement with NSA wasn't a harmless student outreach program. It was a secret intelligence operation intended to combat similar, pro-communist efforts by the Soviet Union and other foreign powers.[184])

Dentzer's career is full of NSA alumni, especially former NSA leaders. While in the CIA, Dentzer worked alongside another former member of the NSA, Bob Kiley. Throughout the 1950s and perhaps much of the 1960s, the NSA appears to have been popular recruiting grounds for the CIA and other important positions in government. NSA alumni often stayed in contact with one another and worked closely in government long after their college days. I point this out mainly to draw attention to the fact that Dentzer had many friends in high places, friends who helped put him in position to become one of Wall Street's most important figures. It's then easy to speculate on how some of Dentzer's CIA friends could have been a part of what took place later.[185]

A second piece of evidence, an old newspaper article, supports the theory that Dentzer might have been involved in top-secret government activities while serving in the CIA, perhaps even covert operations. Here's the context.

On February 26, 1967, the *Los Angeles Times* reported a story about the CIA and its ties to student organizations. The topic of the article was the decade-old mysterious death of a man named S. Avrea Ingram Jr., a former high-ranking member of the National Student Association. Ingram and Dentzer knew each other well and worked closely on numerous NSA projects. For example, as Karen Paget notes in her book, in 1951, while Ingram and Dentzer were still members of the NSA, they submitted "an omnibus funding proposal to President Truman's new Psychological Strategy Board, a group that was intended to coordinate psychological warfare projects across government lines."[186]

After leaving college, Ingram, like Dentzer, joined the International Student Conference in Holland, a student group that had also received funding from the CIA. Ingram spent a large part of the 1950s working for the ISC on CIA-funded, anti-communist student operations in Europe. According to the *Los Angeles Times*, Ingram's final job in Europe was a position as an ISC field worker in Vienna "during and just after the Hungarian uprising of October 1956. His overt job was to help escaping student freedom fighters fleeing Hungary to resettle and resume their studies in the West. What else he may have been doing is not known."[187]

Ingram returned to America and started living at The Inn at Irving Place in New York. Then, at noon on February 5, 1957, a maid found Ingram dead. According to a New York medical examiner, the death was a suicide, but as the *Los Angeles Times* noted, "Some of his friends and relatives were unable to accept that finding."[188]

According to those who knew Ingram, "suicide seemed out of character." The *Los Angeles Times* reported that former NSA officers who knew Ingram said he was "a man who never lost his cool," a "real southern gentleman who loved the fine things in life," and "a bon vivant fond of good food and good times." The *Times* also claimed that it appeared from its investigation that "Ingram was no morose worrier."[189]

Of course, some people who commit suicide show few signs of depression prior to their death. However, the descriptions of Ingram provided by friends and family members are not the only indication that there may be more to this story. The following comes directly from the *Los Angeles Times* report about Ingram's death (one of the declassified documents on the CIA's website). Note how Bill Dentzer's name comes up again:

Right after [Ingram's] funeral, which he attended in Anniston, Ala., Avrea's old friend [William] Dentzer introduced himself to the Ingram family. He took Avrea Jr.'s father and his uncle, Stanton B. Ingram, back to his hotel room, swore them to secrecy and revealed himself as a CIA agent.

Then he said Avrea had also served his country well in intelligence work. Stanton Ingram recalls Dentzer saying,

"If the Communists wanted to kill for their own gain, they would certainly want to kill Avrea Jr. He would be number one on their list."

Ingram's father, a retired businessman, first refused to talk to a reporter about the death of his only child. Later, he said:

"I have been asked not to talk about this death by the government."

But all the recent revelations about the CIA and NSA have caused people to wonder. Carl M. Sapers, an NSA official in 1950-'52 and now a member of the Boston law firm of Hill and Barlow, said in a recent letter to someone in Washington:

"I am now beginning to wonder whether there is not some relation between the CIA involvement and his [Ingram's] death."

For anyone wanting to check the CIA-NSA relationships that have been disclosed now ten years ago, all the links were there.[190]

Adding to the mystery surrounding Ingram's death is the way in which he allegedly committed suicide. When the hotel maid discovered his body, Ingram was lying on the floor completely naked. A leather belt was tied around his neck attached to a dresser drawer.[191] That doesn't sound like a common method of committing suicide— or it sounds like something that might be done by *someone* or some *institution* trying to send a message about Avrea Ingram and his work.

My main interest in this shocking story is the role played by the young CIA officer William Dentzer, the man who would later go on to develop and lead the DTC, one of the most important financial institutions in American history. As I read this account, I had many questions: Why was Dentzer at Ingram's funeral? Was he working with Ingram on covert operations in Europe or in America? Why did Dentzer hint at potential Soviet involvement in Ingram's death? Was the CIA, and perhaps even Dentzer, involved? If so, in what way?

The *Los Angeles Times* article about Ingram's death mentions that Carl Sapers, a man who was also once in the National Student Association, suggested the CIA could be linked to Ingram's death. Sapers certainly knew and had worked closely with Ingram; he likely knew Dentzer personally as well. (Dentzer and Sapers served with the National Student Association around the same period, in the early 1950s.)

I do want to clarify that I'm *not* saying that Dentzer or the CIA was involved in Ingram's death. I'm also *not* suggesting that Ingram was murdered (although murder does seem to be a possibility). My main takeaway from this story is that Dentzer's background was the opposite of what you might expect from someone put in charge of the DTC project.

Dentzer was not a career banker, nor did he have significant experience working on Wall Street. Rather, Dentzer had a long track record of working in international affairs and intelligence operations. As a student, he was part of an organization that opposed communism and received funding from the CIA. After graduating, he joined the CIA, where he apparently continued to be involved in highly sensitive operations. We will likely never know most of what Dentzer did at the CIA, but I believe we can reasonably assume that he and many of the men he knew from his time with the NSA were later engaged in secret intelligence activities at the CIA and elsewhere in the U.S. government.

My main point here is that there is much more to the DTC origin story than first meets the eye, and while Dentzer is not the only prominent figure involved, he is certainly one of the most important. I believe that understanding his background may help to shine some light on the motivations behind the transformation of Wall Street that began in the 1960s and 1970s.

MAKING CONNECTIONS

Following the election of President Kennedy in 1960, Dentzer used a relationship he had with a former NSA member working as a special assistant in the White House to help him transfer out of the CIA into a new government task force. This task force was responsible for starting one of JFK's key foreign policy projects. (If you have been following the actions taken during President Donald Trump's second term in office, you have likely heard of the project. It's called the Agency for International Development, or more commonly, USAID.[192])

Here's how Dentzer described his various roles in government in the early 1960s:

> After John F. Kennedy's election in 1960, I asked one of his White House Special Assistants, a former NSA officer, to arrange my transfer from [the] CIA to the task force that created the Agency for International Development (AID), America's program of foreign assistance to underdeveloped nations. I soon became Special Assistant to the first head of AID, and thereafter Special Assistant to the U.S. Coordinator of the Alliance for Progress, the program initiated by President Kennedy to foster economic development in Latin America.
>
> My work for the Alliance was interrupted by my appointment as Executive Secretary of a committee appointed by President Kennedy and chaired by retired General Lucius Clay. Clay may be best known as the Military Commander in Germany who in 1948 persuaded President Truman to mount the Berlin airlift after Russia blocked land routes to that city. President Kennedy hoped the conservative Clay Committee, which included former World Bank President Eugene Black and Robert Lovett, a former Deputy Secretary of State and Secretary of Defense, would increase Congressional support for AID appropriations. After the committee reported, I followed up as coordinator of AID's annual budget presentation to Congress.[193]

Dentzer's work in the State Department proved to be an important catalyst for his career. The connections he made while working on initiatives like USAID and the Alliance for Progress would become the foundation for Dentzer's bright future at the DTC. In an interview with the SEC Historical Society, Dentzer explained, "It was my relationship with Eugene Black [from the Clay Committee] that, in fact, subsequently, brought me to New York in 1969."[194] The key thing to notice here is that Dentzer's work in the 1960s was essential for his move into domestic policy, and eventually into banking and Wall Street.

Although Dentzer was never the head of either initiative, he played pivotal roles in USAID and the Alliance for Progress. For example, one of Dentzer's responsibilities working for Kennedy's foreign aid task force was helping to select the men who would serve in the top twenty positions in USAID.[195] It might seem strange at first that Dentzer was chosen for such high-level roles in foreign aid programs, but it makes a lot more sense when you take into account how the U.S. government planned to use them.

USAID and the Alliance for Progress were sold as humanitarian efforts (and they did implement many such programs, to be sure), but they were also foreign policy and intelligence tools used by federal government agencies, including the CIA. It's logical, then, that top federal officials would want a former CIA man like Dentzer involved in the rollout of both initiatives.

It's a well-known fact, widely reported for decades, that USAID and the Alliance for Progress were linked to intelligence and other top-secret operations. In a 2014 editorial for *The New York Times*, Peter Kornbluh, the director of the Cuba Documentation Project at the National Security Archive, wrote,

> USAID was created in 1961 to help the United States win the "hearts and minds" of citizens in poor countries through civic action, economic aid and humanitarian assistance. As a Cold War policy tool, the agency was, at times, used as a front for CIA operations and operatives. Among the most infamous examples was the Office of Public Safety, a USAID police training program in the Southern Cone that also trained torturers.[196]

In an article for *Foreign Policy* magazine, Catherine A. Traywick (now a reporter for *Bloomberg News*), wrote,

> Though better known for administering humanitarian aid around the world, USAID has a long history of engaging in intelligence work and meddling in the domestic politics of aid recipients. Throughout the 1960s and 1970s, the agency often partnered with the CIA's now-shuttered Office of Public Safety, a department beset by allegations that it trained foreign police in "terror and torture techniques" and encouraged official brutality, according to a 1976 Government Accountability Office report. USAID officials have always denied these accusations, but in 1973, Congress directed USAID to phase out its public safety program—which worked with the CIA to train foreign police forces—in large part because the accusations were hurting America's public image. "It matters little whether the charges can be substantiated," said a Senate Foreign Relations Committee report. "They inevitably stigmatize the total United States foreign aid effort." By the time the program was closed, USAID had helped train thousands of military personnel and police officers in Vietnam, the Philippines, Indonesia, Thailand, and other countries now notorious for their treatment of political dissidents.[197]

Not only do we know with certainty that Dentzer assisted in the early stages of development of both USAID and the Alliance for Progress, but there is also strong evidence to suggest that he was *directly involved* in intelligence and anti-communist operations while working for the State Department.

In May 1964, the assistant secretary of state for Inter-American Affairs, a high-ranking position in the State Department, sent a "top secret" memo titled "Presidential Election in Chile" to Dean Rusk, the secretary of state under both JFK and Lyndon Johnson. In the memo, the assistant secretary of state for Inter-American Affairs, Thomas C.

Mann, noted that the United States was not only concerned about the rise of a prominent communist political candidate in Chile; is was actively working to undermine him.[198]

"This memorandum will inform you of the status of the presidential race and indicate U.S. Government activity concerning this important election," the memo begins.

The following is a significant portion of the memo. For the sake of space, I have not included the full text; what I have provided, however, will illustrate the sort of work the U.S. government was involved with in Chile in the 1960s. I would advise you to read the following excerpt very carefully:

Situation

On September 4, two months before our own elections, a critical presidential election is scheduled in Chile. The two leading candidates are Salvador Allende, an avowed Marxist leader of a Communist-Socialist coalition, and Eduardo Frei. Frei heads the Christian Democratic Party, a somewhat left of center reform party close to the Catholic Church. In the 1958 election Allende came within 32,000 votes of winning a plurality and becoming president.

At this point in the campaign, most observers rate Frei slightly ahead, but the race will be extremely close and many things could happen in the four months before the election. The democratic forces are presently split, with Radical party candidate Julio Durán back in the race after the results of a congressional bi-election in March shattered his coalition of rightist parties and indicated he stood almost no chance of being elected. Also working against Frei is a Chilean tolerance for native Communists, who have long been on the public scene, and a long-standing anti-clerical feeling which hurts the Church-identified Christian Democrats.

Discussion of U.S. Action Program

Clearly, the September election will be determined by factors which are deeply rooted in the political, economic, and social fabric of the Chilean scene and by the campaign abilities of the major contenders. Given the consequences, however, if this major Latin American nation should become the first country in the hemisphere to freely choose an avowed Marxist as its elected president, the Department, CIA, and other agencies have embarked on a major campaign to prevent Allende's election and to support Frei, the only candidate who has a chance of beating him. Chief elements in this campaign are the following:

1) Providing covert assistance through secret CIA channels to Frei's campaign chest and for other anti-Allende campaign uses. . . .

2) Providing AID loans in CY 64 amounting to approximately $70 million, principally in program budget loans to maintain the level of the government investment budget, thereby keeping the economy as a whole active and unemployment low. $60 million of this aid has already been extended.

3) Examining means to alleviate the rising cost of living through efforts to increase the supply and lower the price of major foods. We are making available $20 million of PL 480, almost half of which is wheat. In addition, we are reviewing our on-going PL 480 Title III food distribution program through voluntary organizations to expand it wherever possible; the current FY 64 program costs $12.5 million and touches an estimated 2 million people, 1/4 of Chile's population.

4) Assisting U.S. business groups with information and advice through David Rockefeller's Business Group for Latin America—a blue ribbon group of American companies in Latin America—in their support of a Chilean business group helping Frei and attempting to hold down prices.

5) Organizing a political action and propaganda campaign through CIA contacts in coordination with or parallel to Frei's campaign. This includes voter registration drives, propaganda, person-to-person campaigning in the cities and rural areas, and arrangements to provide some Italian Christian Democratic organizers to Frei as advisers on campaign techniques. . . .

7) Attempting discreetly through normal U.S. contacts with the non-political Chilean military and police to encourage their rising awareness of the subversion which would take place under an Allende government.

8) Continuing USIA [United States Information Agency] placement in Chile of unattributed material, giving special care to low-keyed efforts which do not expose U.S. government involvement.

9) Encouraging, through covert ties and private U.S. organizations, effective anti-Allende efforts by Chilean organizations including the Roman Catholic Church, trade union groups, and other influential bodies, such as the anti-clerical Masons.
We are attempting to ensure that extraordinary caution is observed in this action campaign to conceal official U.S. government interest, and we have rejected several ideas which have seemed to entail undue risks or excessive American involvement.[199]

That State Department memo leaves no doubt: the CIA and other agencies in the U.S. government were using aid programs, propaganda, and other means to interfere with Chile's election. At the heart of those secret operations was the secretary of Inter-American Affairs, one of the primary offices in charge of the Alliance for Progress.

Where does William Dentzer fit into this? In the first half of the 1960s, Dentzer was the special assistant to Teodoro Moscoso, the head of the Alliance for Progress.[200] And beginning in March 1964, just two months prior to Thomas Mann's "Presidential Election in Chile" memo, Dentzer was appointed the director of the Office of Bolivian-Chilean Affairs, an important part of the Bureau of Inter-American Affairs and the Alliance for Progress.[201] Dentzer wasn't just aware of the top-secret U.S. operations occurring in Chile in 1964. He was actively involved. According to the State Department's Office of the Historian, the Mann memo included above wasn't drafted by Mann. The actual author was William Dentzer.[202]

In 1970, shortly after Dentzer left the State Department, the man he feared would rise to power in Chile—the socialist Salvador Allende—was elected president. Dentzer and other powerful figures in the State Department had successfully helped Eduardo Frei defeat Allende in 1964. By 1970, though, support for socialism had grown, and not even the CIA could stop Allende's ascent to power. However, the U.S. government didn't cease its efforts to covertly battle communism in Chile after Allende's victory. Far from it.

In 1973, a military coup led by General Augusto Pinochet successfully overthrew the Allende-led government. On September 11, Allende delivered his final address to the Chilean people, and then he killed himself. Pinochet ruled Chile with an iron fist for the seventeen years that followed, killing more than three thousand people and holding thirty-eight thousand as political prisoners. Although the U.S. government was not directly linked to the 1973 military coup, it spent millions on secret operations in Chile from 1970 to 1973, all with the intent of undermining Allende and sowing resistance to his communist policies. The sole purpose of those programs was to get Allende out of office as quickly as possible. At one point, the CIA even plotted directly with Chilean military officials to "foment a coup," although that specific operation never materialized.[203]

A MYSTERY IN PERU

In 1965, Dentzer packed his bags and moved his family to Lima, Peru, where he served as the USAID mission director, a position he held until 1968, one year before he moved to New York to join Rockefeller's economic development council.

Dentzer's arrival in Peru came at a pivotal time for the country. In the mid-1960s, Peru was governed by President Fernando Belaúnde Terry, who was first elected in 1963. Belaúnde's administration was considered by U.S. intelligence to be democratic, unlike some others in the region, but it was also marked by mounting economic and political pressures. By 1967, the Peruvian economy had faltered. A severe downturn led to a 31 percent currency devaluation and capital flight. Inflation and budget deficits were rising, undermining public confidence.[204]

Politically, Belaúnde's reform agenda faced obstacles: opposition parties dominated Peru's Congress, frustrating his initiatives. His government was also shaken by corruption scandals implicating high officials, including military officers.[205]

These strains coincided with tensions in the armed forces. The Peruvian military, emboldened by its role in crushing a small leftist guerrilla insurgency in 1965, grew impatient with civilian rule. They pressured Belaúnde to approve big-ticket defense purchases, despite Peru's fiscal troubles. By 1968, many senior officers had lost faith in the civilian government's effectiveness after years of instability and perceived neglect of military interests. The prospect of the left-leaning American Popular Revolutionary Alliance [APRA] party winning the next scheduled elections alarmed the military, which harbored a historic animus toward APRA. Political instability, economic malaise, and military discontent set the stage for a large crisis.[206]

In the midst of this chaos stood Dentzer, USAID mission director (and future head of DTC, one of the world's most important financial institutions). USAID maintained an extensive mission in Peru throughout the 1960s as part of President Kennedy's Alliance for Progress initiative. Under Dentzer's leadership, USAID funded programs aimed at Peru's development, including infrastructure, agriculture, education, and health projects. Similar to other Alliance for Progress efforts, the chief goal of the Peruvian aid programs was to deter the rise of communism.[207]

From World War II until the late 1960s, total U.S. economic aid to Peru grew significantly, reaching about $550 million. Additionally, American aid officials worked closely with Peruvian ministries to implement projects, effectively making USAID an influential actor in Peru's policy sphere.[208]

At the direction of his superiors, Dentzer tied strings to financial support for Belaúnde's government. One of those strings involved the International Petroleum Company (IPC), a subsidiary of Standard Oil of New Jersey. Standard Oil was one of the largest energy companies in the world. It eventually grew and merged with another company to become what it is today—ExxonMobil. The Standard Oil–owned IPC had been in control of valuable, oil-rich lands in Peru since the 1920s, and the business had long been a controversial part of Peruvian politics, with many seeing its operations as exploitive. By the time Dentzer arrived in the 1960s, numerous nationalistic and socialistic Peruvian politicians were calling for the government to seize the oil lands from the IPC, effectively stealing them from Standard Oil of New Jersey.[209, 210]

The IPC controversy proved to be a trigger for a revolution. In 1968, Belaúnde's government signed the Act of Talara, a settlement to resolve IPC's contested oil field concession. The deal would return the La Brea y Pariñas oil fields to the Peruvian state while allowing IPC to retain its refinery and distribution network. However, shortly after the deal was struck, a scandal erupted. A page of the contract between the Peruvian government and IPC was alleged to be missing, fueling suspicions that the Belaúnde administration had given IPC secret favorable terms. This inflamed nationalist sentiment in Peru. In the eyes of many Peruvians, the IPC deal epitomized their government's capitulation to foreign interests.[211]

The Act of Talara was never carried out, because on October 3, 1968, the Peruvian Armed Forces, led by General Juan Velasco Alvarado, executed a swift coup d'état that toppled President Belaúnde's regime. The next day, Velasco canceled the agreement and sent soldiers to occupy the disputed oil fields.[212] Dentzer's USAID and other American operations working in the region failed to keep the IPC in the hands of Standard Oil.

USAID (which includes Dentzer, by extension) was being used as a tool by the American government to protect IPC. Communications between top U.S. officials and the White House made that very clear. In February 1966, Thomas Mann, who was then working as the under secretary of state for economic affairs, wrote a memo to President Lyndon Johnson titled "Aid to Peru and the IPC Problem." In the memo, Mann explained in plain terms how concerns over the confiscation of the IPC oil fields were related to America's willingness to provide humanitarian and economic aid. He also wrote to the president in an attached transmittal note that the IPC situation was a "case study on the difficulties of using aid as a lever to further the national interests."[213]

Here, again, we see Dentzer engaged in important foreign policy work and efforts to interfere in the political affairs of other nations.

But that is not the only reason it's worth discussing Dentzer's time in Peru. His work there might shed light on why he was later chosen to become one of the most powerful bank regulators in America, as well as to run the DTC, despite being very much unqualified for either position.

As mentioned earlier in this chapter, Dentzer, just prior to being put in charge of DTC, served as the New York superintendent of banks. Before that, he worked for the New York Council of Economic Advisers. Both positions required the approval of one man: Nelson Rockefeller. Rockefeller was a progressive Republican and one of America's wealthiest men. He had a keen interest in South American politics and international affairs. An interesting fact to note is that the Rockefeller family was still a major shareholder of Standard Oil of New Jersey at the time Dentzer was trying to protect the IPC (which was, remember, a subsidiary of Standard Oil) from losing its oil fields in Peru.[214]

Dentzer left USAID in 1968, and by 1969, he was working for the New York Council of Economic Advisers.[215, 216] Is it merely a coincidence that Dentzer was involved in helping to protect a Rockefeller company under attack just one year before being brought to New York to serve a Rockefeller in a position for which he was apparently unqualified? Maybe. However, it seems likely that Nelson Rockefeller selected Dentzer in part because of his service to the Rockefeller family's interests.

Another strange part of the Dentzer Peru story is Dentzer's explanation for why he left his role as head of USAID in Peru in 1968: "I worked thereafter in the State Department and became the AID mission director in Peru, 1965 to '68. I came back in 1968 on my own initiative because I 'knew' that Nixon would beat Humphrey, and as a Democrat, I knew, I would be put out to pasture. So I came back to the United States to be sure the pasture was a U.S. pasture rather than a Peruvian pasture."[217]

For those who don't know their Peruvian history, that sounds like a reasonable explanation. However, Dentzer curiously left out something very important, as we have discussed at length in this chapter: the military coup and the negative impact that it had on the relationship between the United States and Peru. It seems strange that Dentzer would say that Nixon was his primary motivation for leaving his post and restarting his career in a completely new field, rather than the political earthquake that happened that same year in Peru. (Even if Dentzer resigned from his position before the coup, which is a possibility, since I have been unable to discover the exact date of his departure, he must have known that trouble was brewing in the country and that the trouble would be more concerning than an upcoming presidential election.) It's especially odd because Dentzer, a Democrat, later went to work for a Republican, Rockefeller, who also had close ties to President Nixon.

There may be perfectly reasonable explanations, but you must admit that, at the very least, it's odd that Dentzer didn't mention the difficulties on the ground in Peru when explaining his reasons for leaving USAID, an organization he helped build.

It has made me wonder if Dentzer didn't want anyone asking questions about what he was up to while running USAID in Peru.

BACK TO THE BEGINNING

At the start of this chapter, I provided a brief review of how DTC came into existence: Throughout the 1960s, large financial institutions developed plans and tested methods for centralizing the ownership of securities. In the early 1970s, powerful industry leaders approached Dentzer, who had just left his job as the top bank regulator in New York, and asked him to run one of the most important projects in Wall Street's history.

That raised many questions: Why Dentzer? Why not someone with far more experience in banking, or someone who had worked on Wall Street, or someone who knew something about how securities transactions worked? Why a CIA man who spent nearly two decades involved in covert activities and secret plans?

In his 2011 interview with the SEC Historical Society, Dentzer explained that in the early years of DTC, he was the chairman and CEO, but he was not DTC's president. Instead, Dentzer says a man named Diran Kaloostian was chosen for the role. The following is how Dentzer described the decision. (Pay special attention to the reason Kaloostian was needed as president in DTC's first days.)

> Diran was the operations head of CCS [the Central Certificate Service] within the Clearing Corporation of the New York Stock Exchange, and really was running this embryonic depository, which had some deposits of broker-dealer securities after it was turned on in the late 1960s. The deal with me was they would hire me if I would hire Diran as the president. Well, since I knew nothing about securities, securities custody, securities law and computers, I was only too happy to hire Diran because he was knowledgeable on these subjects. We began then in '72. By '74, I had learned the ropes, and I had reached the conclusion that Diran would have to go. He did some things that suggested to me that I really couldn't trust his judgment.[218]

According to Dentzer's own words, he "knew nothing about securities, securities custody, securities law and computers." *Nothing.* Does he sound like the right man to run an innovative, high-stakes new securities venture to you?

Even more remarkable, Dentzer had been embroiled in a large scandal in his final years with USAID. In 1967, a publication called *Ramparts* magazine published an exposé of the CIA's involvement with the National Student Association. Prior to 1967, the public did not know that the CIA had been funding and working alongside one of America's largest student organizations, as well as using the NSA as a recruiting ground for new officers. The backlash was intense. Americans suddenly realized they had been misled into believing the CIA meddled only in the affairs of other countries, not their own.[219]

Dentzer publicly defended the CIA's involvement with the NSA, even going so far as to issue a press release with other former NSA presidents that claimed that although the group had accepted money from the CIA, it had always operated independently.[220]

One would think that Dentzer's loyalty would have earned him better treatment from the CIA. Not so. At the height of the scandal, CIA Director Richard Helms told *The New York Times* that Dentzer had asked the CIA for the funding, that it wasn't the CIA's idea to give the NSA money; it was Dentzer's. It was an audacious claim, one that Dentzer would deny repeatedly later in life.[221, 222]

Regardless of who initially came up with the idea to have the CIA secretly fund a popular American student organization, the fact is that the story about Dentzer broke years *before* he had been recruited for the job with the New York Council of Economic Advisers, the position as New York's top bank regulator, and the role as head of DTC. Considering how unpopular the CIA's program was, one would think the news would have made Dentzer an even less desirable choice for these jobs (roles he didn't seem qualified for in the first place). However, the scandal appeared to have little, if any, negative effect on his career prospects.

LET'S SPECULATE WILDLY

In my opinion—and, obviously, this is speculative—there are two good theories for why Dentzer was chosen for his positions in New

York and with the DTC. And neither has anything to do with him being the most qualified person available. Clearly, he was not.

First, it's possible Dentzer was selected because the elites in the banking industry wanted someone with a background like Dentzer's to run their new project. Yes, he didn't know anything about securities or banking, but he did know how to accomplish complex missions on tight deadlines. He also knew how to keep secrets, a valuable skill when setting up an institution designed to undermine individuals' property rights.

Perhaps Dentzer's time in Peru caught the attention of the Rockefellers. They were major players in New York and in the banking industry when Dentzer was chosen to lead DTC. Nelson's brother, David, was a larger-than-life figure who had worked for years in banking, eventually becoming the head of Chase Manhattan Bank. While serving as president of Chase, the bank helped develop one of the early pilot programs for centralizing the ownership and control of securities.[223] It's not hard to imagine why they might have selected Dentzer, given his background as a defender of Rockefeller oil interests.

It's also reasonable to think that Dentzer's time working with Eugene Black played a vital role in his meteoric rise. Black and Dentzer knew each other from their time serving on a committee created by President John F. Kennedy to drum up support for USAID, and Dentzer says it was Black who recruited him to New York in 1969.[224]

Like Rockefeller, Black was a notable figure in banking. He had worked for a time at Chase, as did Rockefeller, and was the head of the World Bank from 1949 to 1963. He was a prominent adviser to presidents, including Lyndon Johnson. Black was intimately involved in global development financing, one of the primary ways the United States sought to coerce developing countries to adopt anti-communist policies.

Black knew the Rockefellers. They shared similar, progressive views. They ran in many of the same circles, both in business and public policy. If Black vouched for Dentzer, I suspect that held great weight with people like Nelson and David Rockefeller.

All of this begs the question, Were Black and the Rockefellers the masterminds behind the creation of DTC? I think the answer must be that, while far from proven, it's possible. We know the Rockefeller brothers and Black were heavily involved in banking and public policy at the time DTC was created. We also know that David Rockefeller's Chase Manhattan Bank was one of the earliest proponents of centralizing ownership of securities. Their progressive ideological views fit well with the goals of DTC, and the Rockefellers were masters of using their financial might to push for public policy changes. The fact that Nelson Rockefeller and Eugene Black were both involved in bringing Dentzer to New York in the first place is strong evidence that they might have been behind the DTC plot.

However, there are several good reasons not to believe that this is the case. First, I couldn't find any available records suggesting that Black supported DTC or even mentioned it publicly. There are also no publicly available records showing that Nelson Rockefeller supported DTC or the development of a similar institution. Most importantly, in my opinion, there is at least one source who claims that David Rockefeller's Chase Manhattan Bank ended up being one of the "big holdouts" in agreeing to implement the DTC model, even though it appears Chase Bank was an early supporter of the plan.[225]

In a 2011 interview with the SEC Historical Society, William Jaenike, a former DTC chairman and CEO, was asked how DTC managed to convince banks and other financial institutions to turn over all of their securities certificates when the idea was still relatively new.

"There was a lot of pressure from the brokers. 'We want you to take book-entry delivery from us brokers, and once you try it, you're going to like it. It's so efficient and it's so safe,'" Jaenike said. "Then one of the big holdouts in this whole story was, of all banks, David Rockefeller's bank, Chase. There was a senior executive there at the time who was very skeptical of the safety of DTC. He had been told by his staff, 'What happens if, somehow or other, DTC is penetrated, either from the bookkeeping system or from the physical assets? We'll be out of luck. If we have our securities in there, what happens then?'"[226]

Of course, Chase eventually caved, and Jaenike's story never says Rockefeller himself opposed the plan. It stands to reason, though, that if David Rockefeller were one of the driving forces behind DTC, no one from his own bank would be so brazen about opposing it.

A second, more troubling theory is that Dentzer was chosen because figures in the White House, State Department, or perhaps even the CIA were involved and wanted one of their own men to be in leadership of DTC. This theory may sound ridiculous, but it best resolves the issue of Dentzer's lack of experience. If the CIA or another important agency were pushing for DTC, it would make sense to have someone like Dentzer at the top of the organization.

Under this theory, it is also possible that Dentzer was picked because private industry leaders could trust him; because of his connections to Black and his work to protect the IPC in Peru and figures in government; because of his work in the State Department and CIA.

Why would the CIA or some other government agency want to create or be involved in the creation of something like DTC? Well, there was likely not as much for them to gain from the change to a centralized ownership model as there was for large banks and brokers, but progressives in government almost always prefer centralization of power and wealth over decentralization. If nearly all securities are directly owned by a single institution, they become easier to control. Centralizing registered ownership of securities also means that they can be utilized, if necessary, in the event of a catastrophic event that crushes the U.S. economy, like a nuclear war, for example.

I cannot confirm that Dentzer and DTC were part of a larger plot that involved the CIA or other government agencies, but if I could, I wouldn't be surprised. Not only did Dentzer have a long track record of engaging in top-secret government activities (as I have shown throughout this chapter), he had personal connections to some of the most important figures in the CIA at the time he was recruited to lead the DTC.

Bob Kiley, for example, was the manager of intelligence operations and then executive assistant to CIA Director Richard Helms before leaving the agency in 1970.[227] If the CIA were involved in the creation of DTC, the wheels would likely have been in motion before Kiley's departure. Kiley had a long history with Dentzer. Not only did they both serve in the CIA, but they also were former NSA presidents who helped the CIA continue to facilitate its relationship with NSA long after the two men graduated from college.[228]

Of Dentzer's CIA connections, the most interesting to me is Cord Meyer Jr., a decorated World War II veteran who had lost an eye fighting the Japanese in the Pacific theater. Meyer was from a wealthy family, a graduate of Yale, and a former advocate of global governance (a position he later repudiated). Meyer joined the CIA in 1951, just after the agency started funding the National Student Association.[229]

In the mid-1950s, Meyer was put in charge of the NSA-CIA program. Although Dentzer was no longer president when Meyer took over, the two worked together on various NSA-related activities. It appears that Meyer was in charge of or working on the NSA-CIA operation throughout Dentzer's time in the agency.[230]

As *The Washington Post* noted in Cord Meyer's obituary, he went on to become one of the CIA's most influential figures. "He advanced to become the top deputy in a section of the agency called the 'dirty tricks department' by detractors because of its elaborate activities aimed at curbing communist influence." Meyer ran numerous covert operations and propaganda efforts while serving in the CIA, including key programs related to Radio Free Europe / Radio Liberty.[231]

Meyer has also been a frequent topic of conversation among investigators of the JFK assassination. Meyer married Mary Pinchot Meyer shortly after the end of World War II. Mary Meyer divorced Cord in 1958 and later developed a sexual affair with JFK. She and Cord knew the Kennedy family personally. JFK and Jackie Kennedy lived next door to the Meyers in the 1950s in McLean, Virginia, and Mary Meyer had known JFK in high school.[232]

The affair lasted from at least the early 1960s to JFK's death in November 1963. Less than a year after Kennedy was assassinated, in October 1964, Mary Meyer was also murdered in broad daylight while walking along a towpath in Georgetown. The towpath was a popular destination for pedestrians and bicyclists, and thus a strange place to murder a well-known woman.[233] The killer was never found.

Mary Meyer's death has fueled speculation for decades that she may have been assassinated by figures tied to JFK's murder. Perhaps Cord Meyer himself was involved. He was, after all, a top man in the CIA at the time, and he most likely wasn't happy that his former neighbor, JFK, was having an affair with his ex-wife. If Cord Meyer wanted to kill JFK or Mary Meyer (or both), he would have known how to do it without getting caught.

I have not been able to find any direct evidence that Cord Meyer or the CIA was involved in the creation of DTC. But one thing is clear: the person who helped create and lead DTC for two decades, William Dentzer, was unquestionably a CIA man with a long track record of engaging in secret government programs, and he had many high-ranking friends in the CIA at the time the DTC plan was in development. These could be coincidences, but they could just as easily be evidence of a deliberate plan.

WHAT WE KNOW

What do we know for certain about the creation of DTC and the centralization of securities? We know that investors' property rights have been taken away. We know that in the midst of a large economic crash, it's possible for the federal government to put people's securities at risk and that, if the financial collapse were big enough, tens of millions of people could lose everything. We also know that in situations where broker-dealers improperly use their customers' securities investments as collateral, customers are at risk of losing their investments.

We know that William Dentzer helped create DTC and developed the institution into one of the most important Wall Street entities ever devised. We know that Dentzer was a CIA man who worked for years in South America on top-secret programs. We know that Dentzer helped the Rockefellers in Peru and then soon after got a job working for a Rockefeller economic policy commission, despite having no domestic policy experience. We know Dentzer was then quickly named the head bank regulator of New York by Nelson Rockefeller, despite Dentzer's lack of knowledge or experience in banking, and then, shortly after that, he was put in charge of DTC, a position he was not qualified for at all.

We know that throughout the 1960s and 1970s, key figures in the CIA and American politics, who knew Dentzer well, rose to power. If the CIA or another government agency wanted to involve itself in the DTC scheme, Dentzer would be a logical choice to help.

There is much that is known about DTC, but the truth is, we will likely never discover all the facts behind its creation. However, we don't need to understand how DTC came into existence to make the changes needed to protect people from a future economic crisis. In the final chapter of this book, we'll discuss steps that individuals can take to guard against the dangers posed by the DTC system, as well as additional legislative safeguards that lawmakers could enact to help avert a future disaster.

For now, know that solutions do exist, and there are many men and women today fighting to make them happen (including the author of this book).

In the next chapter, we'll turn our attention to the potential impact that a major economic crisis could have on America's currency. DTC's potential impact on your life could prove to be limited in comparison to the problems that could arise if the United States were to adopt a central bank digital currency—and there are plenty of reasons to believe that it soon will.

4

THE DIGITAL DOLLAR DILEMMA: HOW A CBDC COULD RESHAPE AMERICA IN THE WAKE OF COLLAPSE

Economic crises often serve as accelerators for long imagined reforms and expansions of government power. In the event that the next big economic crash shakes the foundations of the U.S. financial system, it's likely that the federal government could significantly increase its influence and authority over our everyday lives via the launch of a central bank digital currency (CBDC).

According to the Federal Reserve's FAQ, "A CBDC is a digital form of central bank money that is widely available to the general public."[234]

Unlike nearly all money in existence today, one of the central features of CBDCs are that they do *not* exist physically. They are solely digital: they operate only in electronic form.

CBDCs are not digital versions of physical cash. They are entirely new currencies that operate separately from a country's physical currency (although it *is* possible to tie the value of a CBDC to a physical currency).

A CBDC is often linked with cryptocurrencies and does share some features with popular cryptos like Bitcoin, such as having a digital design.[235] However, the implementation and management of a CBDC are radically different than that of cryptocurrencies, which are usually controlled by private companies or individual citizens. Additionally, cryptocurrencies are typically, though not always, built using a decentralized blockchain network.

A CBDC is issued and controlled by the state or central banks. In the United States, the monetary authority given control of a U.S. CBDC, whether the Federal Reserve or another organization, would have the power to design the CBDC's functionality. Because a CBDC is digital, it offers governments and central banks significantly more options than physical currencies for how it is designed, such as the abilities to control where it is spent and how much can be transferred in one transaction.

It is likely that, if the United States implemented a CBDC, in the early days government and banking authorities would promote it as a solution to restore order, provide financial stability, and rebuild trust in a broken monetary system. A CBDC is typically framed in language that is appealing to both technocrats and reformers, using terms like *financial inclusion, payment efficiency, fraud reduction,* and *innovation.* Underneath, however, is a policy tool that is capable of transforming the relationship between citizens and the state.

In short, it is my opinion that a CBDC is one of the greatest threats to freedom in America today. If the authority controlling the

CBDC can manipulate how, where, and when people spend money, it can control just about everything else in the process. Digital, programmable currencies provide the opportunity to governments and central bankers to micromanage society in a way that no other technology has in the past.

This might sound like science fiction, but as I'll present later in this chapter, the U.S. government, Federal Reserve, and their think tank allies have already spent a substantial amount of time and energy studying the feasibility of a CBDC, planning how it could be rolled out, debating potential design options, and even worrying about its impact on the environment. President Joe Biden gave orders to many of the larger federal agencies to produce reports specifically about the benefits and risks of a CBDC.[236] This is something that could occur only if many in Washington were serious about eventually imposing a new CBDC.

It does seem certain that a CBDC is coming, although it's very probable that lawmakers will wait for a future crisis to occur before suggesting a sweeping overhaul to America's monetary system. The creation of a new CBDC will be a controversial move when it's finally released, and the perfect crisis for such a transformation could be the next big crash.

In this chapter, I will explore how crises empower state actors to implement schemes, such as a CBDC, to gain power. I will further investigate the ideological, political, and technological forces driving CBDC development in the United States and abroad, with an emphasis on how CBDCs would likely be embedded with policy objectives and other goals of the ruling class. As part of that endeavor, I will provide readers with evidence to show that a U.S.-based CBDC would, if fully implemented, open the door to a surveillance-based, behavior-modifying currency system.

History teaches us that moments of national panic are rarely wasted by those in power. The same urgency that compels the public to accept bold solutions can also be harnessed to bring about changes that, under normal circumstances, would be fiercely resisted. In the pages that follow, I hope to show you what a CBDC truly represents: a potential turning point in the balance between individual liberty and state control.

HOW THE NEXT CRASH COULD TRIGGER A CBDC ROLLOUT

In a major economic crash, trust in traditional banks, fiat money, and the Federal Reserve could collapse, especially if Americans find themselves unable to access cash, credit cards, or digital payment platforms. Regardless of the reasons behind the crash, Americans will almost certainly seek quick and efficient government relief, like in most modern political systems. A CBDC, due to its versatility, will almost certainly be pitched as a potential solution to the financial crisis. It would be particularly appealing in the context of a dire economic crisis, since a digital currency can be created and distributed rapidly, unlike physical dollars, which take time for the government to create and move through the banking system.

Imagine with me how things might play out. In the event of a massive economic crash, Congress might authorize emergency CBDC digital wallets to every American adult. These digital wallets could receive direct stimulus payments, perhaps through a Federal Reserve app, to help citizens survive in a crisis, or perhaps to keep the economy from collapsing further. The public, desperate for stability, would likely sign up en masse. The result could be nearly all Americans finding themselves trapped in a state-controlled financial system, unlike anything they have experienced before.

When a currency is digital and programmable, anything is possible. Controls could be introduced incrementally: spending limits, expiration dates for funds (to stimulate the economy), and restrictions on "nonessential" purchases. These policies may initially seem reasonable, but the structure, once built, would likely be permanent. Every dollar you earn, save, or spend could be tracked, controlled, and conditioned. China has already demonstrated this model with its digital yuan. As I will show later in this chapter, the digital yuan is, by design, an authoritarian tool of the Chinese Communist Party, with the primary purpose of helping the CCP better control the Chinese populace.[237]

U.S. advocates of a CBDC claim their version would allow for much greater freedom and privacy than China's. There are, however, few reasons to trust that the U.S. government or Federal Reserve would limit themselves if given the opportunity to expand their influence and power. U.S. history has taught us this lesson.

HISTORICAL PRECEDENTS: CRISIS AS A CATALYST FOR GOVERNMENT POWER

Let's take a look back at our history to help us understand the danger of a CBDC rollout in the aftermath of a crash. Over and over, periods of national crisis in the United States have been used to justify large expansions of federal power, and many of those expansions remained long after the emergency passed.

Consider the New Deal. In the wake of the Great Depression, President Franklin D. Roosevelt's administration redefined the federal government's role in American life. Through a flurry of new programs and agencies, Washington took on responsibilities that had once been unthinkable at the federal level: unemployment insurance, welfare payments, agricultural price supports, public housing, and immense infrastructure projects. Critics at the time warned that these moves were unconstitutional and eroded personal responsibility. But the public, reeling from the collapse of markets and banks, accepted the trade-off: security in exchange for some of their freedom.

That trade-off was not temporary. What began as emergency intervention quickly solidified into permanent government architecture. Social Security, for example, was signed into law in 1935 as a modest retirement benefit. Today, it is the nation's largest and costliest federal program.[238] Regardless of whether you think Social Security is a beneficial program, there's no question that it started because of a crisis and that the majority of older Americans are now completely dependent on it.

Of course, social welfare programs and an expanding bureaucratic state were not the only expansions of governmental power during the Roosevelt years. Following Japan's attack on Pearl Harbor during World War II, the entire West Coast of the United States was declared a military area. Then, using the authority granted by Roosevelt's Executive Order 9066, military commanders began imposing curfews that applied only to Japanese Americans.[239]

In 1942, the authoritarianism of the Roosevelt administration increased, as the National Archives records:

On March 29, 1942, under the authority of the [Roosevelt] executive order, [Lieutenant General John L.] DeWitt issued Public Proclamation No. 4, which began the forced evacuation and detention of Japanese American West Coast residents on a 48-hour notice. Only a few days prior to the proclamation, on March 21, Congress had passed Public Law 503, which made violation of Executive Order 9066 a misdemeanor punishable by up to one year in prison and a $5,000 fine.

Because of the perception of "public danger," all Japanese Americans within varied distances from the Pacific Coast were targeted. Unless they were able to dispose of or make arrangements for care of their property within a few days, their homes, farms, businesses, and most of their private belongings were lost forever.

From the end of March to August, approximately 112,000 persons were sent to "assembly centers"—often racetracks or fairgrounds—where they waited and were tagged to indicate the location of a long-term "relocation center" that would be their home for the rest of the war. Nearly 70,000 of the evacuees were American citizens. There were no charges of disloyalty against any of these citizens, nor was there any vehicle by which they could appeal their loss of property and personal liberty.[240]

Roosevelt is not the only president who expanded his authority in the midst of a crisis. Fast forward to the post-9/11 era. The trauma of the terrorist attacks gave birth to the PATRIOT Act, one of the country's largest expansions of surveillance and law enforcement. In the name of national security, the federal government granted itself broad authority to monitor communications, temporarily detain individuals without trial, and collect vast amounts of data. Some of these measures were later reined in, but many remain to this day, and new programs, such as warrantless surveillance of metadata, were quietly increased.[241]

Transformations to the country's monetary systems have also historically come in the wake of large crises. World War II, one of the most destructive periods in human history, was the setting for the Bretton Woods Conference, which created many of the most important international monetary institutions operating today and made the U.S. dollar the world's reserve currency.[242] Bretton Woods would never have occurred had Europe not been devastated and dependent on America. I will explain the Bretton Woods Conference in more detail later in this chapter.

In all these examples, the common theme is crisis. When people are afraid of starvation, collapse, economic turmoil, or violence, they are more likely to accept government control, which they would otherwise reject. As Rahm Emanuel, President Barack Obama's former chief of staff, famously put it, "You never want a serious crisis to go to waste."[243]

A CBDC fits neatly into this pattern. In the wake of an economic crash (especially one involving the collapse of multiple banks or a widespread failure of payment systems), it seems very likely to me that many in the federal government will argue that only a programmable, secure, and centrally issued digital dollar will be able to restore public confidence and keep the economy functioning. Like the New Deal or the PATRIOT Act, a CBDC would likely begin with limited, targeted goals, such as emergency payments, stabilization, and fraud prevention, but it would be simple for those limits to expand quickly. Features that would initially be touted as conveniences, like programmability, expiration dates, and spending categories, could eventually become tools of social control.

This is why it's important for Americans to understand the political and historical pattern that it fits into.

THE GLOBAL PUSH FOR CBDCs

Although the United States does not yet have a CBDC, officials in other countries around the world are not waiting for an economic crash. They have already started to launch CBDC pilot programs and construct international financial infrastructure designed specifically for the widespread use of digital currencies. First among them is China.

Understanding China's CBDC

The country that has perhaps made the biggest strides toward full adoption of a CBDC is China. Over the past several years, it has instituted large-scale pilot programs for its digital yuan, known as the e-CNY, across more than twenty cities and more than a dozen provinces. As of 2022, 261 million Chinese citizens had set up a digital yuan wallet, which they use for everyday transactions, from public transit to buying groceries. Far from hypothetical, China's CBDC is public policy in action. The lessons it offers are chilling.[244]

The People's Bank of China (PBOC) has made its purpose clear: the e-CNY is central to the country's long-term strategy for economic modernization, national security, and social governance. The currency's most notable feature is its programmability. The government can assign expiration dates to funds, restrict where money can be spent, and even limit what kinds of goods can be purchased, although the extent to which this is already occurring is anybody's guess. The Chinese government treats its digital yuan as a work in progress and has not revealed exactly how the government is using its programmable features.[245]

One of the earliest and most publicized pilots occurred in Shenzhen in 2020. Citizens, selected via lottery, received digital "red envelopes" filled with e-CNY. They could spend this money only at designated merchants and within a fixed time frame. While marketed as a consumer stimulus initiative, the pilot embedded the foundational mechanisms of a programmable CBDC: geographic limitations, use-it-or-lose-it deadlines, and retail surveillance.[246]

In December 2020, the Chinese government instituted another large pilot program in Suzhou, issuing one hundred thousand digital red packets worth 20 million yuan (about $3 million). While the pilot was officially aimed at boosting consumption during a major shopping festival, it demonstrated the government's ability to program monetary behavior, setting a precedent for a system in which authorities could potentially guide not just how much money individuals receive but also when and where it must be spent.[247]

Since the end of those pilot programs, the Chinese government has launched numerous other digital yuan programs in cities such as

Beijing, Changshu, Chengdu, Dalian, Shenzhen, Shanghai, Qingdao, Xi'an, and Xiong'an.[248, 249] These digital yuan programs and a long list of official statements vividly illustrate that the Chinese Communist Party's long-term goal is for widespread use and adoption. Because the Chinese people have little choice but to accept the CCP's agenda, a growing share of China's economic system will soon be funneled into a state-run, selectively programmable currency regime, which comes with significant risks. Based on its previous track record, the Chinese Communist Party will likely abuse its power over China's CBDC.

The Communist Party already has in place an immense social credit scoring scheme that it uses to manipulate the behavior of the Chinese people. China's social credit system is a government-led framework designed to monitor and evaluate the trustworthiness of individuals, businesses, and organizations by aggregating data from financial records, legal compliance, social behavior, and other sources. Using both public and private sector inputs, the system assigns scores or classifications that can affect a person's or entity's access to services, loans, employment opportunities, and more.[250, 251, 252]

Social credit systems have been planned or trialed in roughly 80 percent of all Chinese regions over the past two decades. In a report published by *Newsweek*, John Feng provided details about how some of the programs work:

Primary sources fed into these systems include familiar datapoints such as financial records and dealings with lenders. Beyond that, however, local governments have been given the freedom to experiment, devising their own prizes and penalties.

Remaining debt-free and volunteering for community service were two ways of boosting one's social credit score in some localities. Benefits of maintaining a positive profile included priority health care and deposit-free rental of public housing.

On the opposite end of the spectrum, sanctions for low creditworthiness included a ban on applying for public sector jobs and difficulty accessing home mortgage loans. Some pilots restricted government officials to economy-class seats on flights and trains, or prohibited them from buying property.[253]

Feng further reported, "Some of the most controversial trials included one in Rongcheng, a city of 710,000 people. Officials there assigned each resident 1,000 social credit points, which would increase or decrease depending on behavior—jaywalking or littering, for instance."[254]

"China's central bank estimated that just over 1 billion individuals—around 70 percent of the population—were covered by the social credit system by the end of 2019," and by July of the same year, millions had already been punished for having a low social credit rating.[255]

According to Feng, citing the National Development and Reform Commission, "2.5 million people across the country had been barred from flights, 90,000 people had been restricted from high-speed rail services, and 300,000 people had been deemed untrustworthy by Chinese courts."[256]

A CBDC has yet to be fully implemented, but once it is combined with China's authoritarian social credit scoring system, whatever freedoms the Chinese people may have will be quickly obliterated.

I'm not the only one who has sounded this alarm. In an article for the Cato Institute, James A. Dorn summarized some of the major concerns about the digital yuan, citing numerous scholars and researchers. According to Dorn,

It would be foolish to think that there is a zero probability that China would never abolish cash or that the privacy afforded by physical cash could be approximated by "managed anonymity" under a digital yuan regime. So, while it is true that digitizing cash and coins would reduce the costs of issuing fiat money—as Fan Yifei, deputy governor of the PBOC, has argued—it is also true that a digital yuan would diminish individual freedom.

Alex Gladstein, chief strategy officer at the Human Rights Foundation, has recognized the danger to financial freedom and privacy inherent in central bank digital currency (CBDC), especially in repressive regimes like China. According to Gladstein, "The end of cash and the insta-analysis of financial transactions enable surveillance, state control, and, eventually, social engineering on a scale never thought possible." He points to China's social credit system, in conjunction with a digital yuan, as paving the way toward "financial omniscience." Thus,

> When the government can take financial privileges away for posting the wrong word on social media, saying the wrong thing in a call to parents, or sending the wrong photo to relatives, individuals self-censor and exercise extreme caution. In this way, control over money can create a social chilling effect.

It is instructive, as Andrew Liu has reported in the *Cato Journal*, that government authorities have used regulations on mobile payments "to help the Communist Party maintain full political, social, and economic power," even though the official rhetoric is that those regulations were intended "to prevent criminal activity and improve mobile payment security." There is little doubt that Xi Jinping and his cadres in the State Council will be tempted to politicize the digital yuan to serve their own interests.[257]

China's digital currency program is more than an economic experiment. It fits beautifully into the Communist Party's vision of a managed society, where behavior, access, and opportunity are distributed based on compliance, not by markets or on merit.

You may not live in China, but these developments will affect you whether you live in that country or not. The more successful and normalized China's social credit scoring and adoption of digital currencies have become, the more rapidly both systems have been pursued by institutions in Western nations.

The West's Move Toward CBDCs

Today, influential organizations like the World Economic Forum (WEF), think tanks, and governments like the European Union are actively shaping the conversation around CBDCs, both within their own jurisdictions as well as on the international stage. While these institutions do not have direct power over U.S. law, their ideas and partnerships increasingly inform the direction of central banking and global finance. They don't control monetary policy in America, but they work closely with U.S. politicians and the leaders of the Federal Reserve who do.

The WEF has emerged as a powerful global cheerleader for CBDCs.[258] While it presents itself as a neutral platform for dialogue between public and private sectors, the WEF's messaging around digital currencies has consistently emphasized goals aligned with progressive governance: inclusion, sustainability, and global cooperation.[259] WEF authors have routinely downplayed the threats of a CBDC, although there are many in the WEF who acknowledge that threats exist, at least to some extent.[260]

Another powerful institution advancing the CBDC agenda is the International Monetary Fund (IMF). The IMF is a global financial institution, established in 1944 at the Bretton Woods Conference in New Hampshire. The Bretton Woods Conference was a landmark event in the history of global economic governance. It laid the foundation for the post–World War II international financial system. Representatives from dozens of Allied nations attended the conference, with the primary goal of restructuring the global economy and preventing a recurrence of the economic disasters that preceded World War II, especially the Great Depression. The conference was one of the most important economic events in world history. It is most famous for setting up a system of fixed exchange rates, where countries pegged their currencies to the U.S. dollar, and the dollar was convertible to gold at $35 per ounce. This made the U.S. dollar the central reserve currency in the global economy.[261]

Leaders at the Bretton Woods Conference, primarily driven by a progressive ideological agenda, created the IMF to promote international monetary cooperation and ensure the stability of the global financial system. For the IMF to work, further financial and economic centralization was needed.

One of the IMF's primary goals is to promote international monetary cooperation by providing a forum for consultation and collaboration on international financial issues. Other goals are ensuring exchange rate stability, avoiding competitive devaluations, and facilitating the balanced growth of international trade (which contributes to high employment and real income levels). The organization also lends to member countries facing balance-of-payments problems, often to stabilize their economies and restore growth, and works to reduce global poverty, especially through concessional lending to low-income countries.[262]

The IMF offers technical assistance and training in areas like fiscal policy, monetary and exchange rate policy, regulatory frameworks, and economic statistics to help countries build strong institutions and policymaking capacity. Needless to say, the IMF is one of the most influential institutions in global finance.

The IMF has not only supported the use of CBDCs; it has actively taken steps to make Cbdcs a reality. In 2023, Reuters reported, "The International Monetary Fund (IMF) is working on a platform for central bank digital currencies (Cbdcs) to enable transactions between countries, IMF Managing Director Kristalina Georgieva said on Monday."[263] Georgieva might not be a household name, but she's a powerful figure in international affairs and a committed globalist. She has also been a prominent supporter of the WEF's Great Reset initiative, participating in the program's launch event.[264] (The Great Reset is an economic recovery plan launched in 2020 as a response to the COVID-19 pandemic.)

There are some influential American policy organizations who have been pushing for the adoption of a CBDC. One prominent example is the Atlantic Council, a major player in Washington, D.C., and abroad. The Atlantic Council has a $70 million budget (a large figure for a think tank) and even greater influence. It regularly participates in many of the biggest international forums, and its prominent list of board members, staffers, and policy experts include Robert M. Gates, a former secretary of defense and CIA director; Stephen Hadley, the national security adviser for President George W. Bush; and Condoleezza Rice, another former secretary of state and also a national security adviser.[265]

The Atlantic Council has hosted CBDC-themed events, has published policy papers on Cbdcs, and regularly engages with policymakers and central bankers as part of its effort to help design and normalize the adoption of Cbdcs in Western countries.[266]

With the support of these and many other important institutions, a number of central banks around the world have started the process of designing an official CBDC. According to the Atlantic Council, "134 countries & currency unions, representing 98% of global GDP, are exploring a CBDC. In May 2020 that number was only 35. Currently, 66 countries are in the advanced phase of exploration—development, pilot, or launch."[267]

As of June 2025, "There is a new high of 44 ongoing CBDC pilots, including the digital euro. European countries—both in the euro area and beyond—are increasingly testing wholesale CBDCs, both domestically and across borders."[268]

As the Atlantic Council report goes on to state, "Every G20 country is exploring a CBDC, with 19 of them in the advanced stages of CBDC exploration. Of those, 13 countries are already in the pilot stage. This includes Brazil, Japan, India, Australia, Russia, and Turkey."[269]

AMERICAN CBDC PROJECTS

What about the United States? In most countries, there has been relatively little resistance to CBDCs, but many Americans are deeply worried about their development. CBDCs raise serious privacy and liberty concerns, and Americans, more than most other populations, are skeptical of government and Federal Reserve programs that could limit individual rights.

An official, consumer-focused CBDC program has not been created in the United States and likely won't be under the Trump administration. President Trump and many of his officials are on record saying they completely oppose a CBDC, and in January 2025, the White House issued an executive order that bans federal agencies from taking any action to promote or create a CBDC.[270]

Despite the resistance from President Trump, many members of the American ruling class, on both sides of the aisle, have been quietly working for years to make a CBDC a reality. If the right circumstances were to arise in the future, such as a wide-scale economic crash, policymakers and central bankers would almost certainly try to impose a CBDC, and there's a good chance that whatever CBDC emerged would be used to restrict many of the freedoms we enjoy.

The United States has seen the launch of a number of CBDC-related research projects, such as Project Hamilton, a research initiative jointly conducted by the Federal Reserve Bank of Boston and the Massachusetts Institute of Technology's Digital Currency Initiative. Launched in 2020, the project aimed to explore the technical feasibility of a CBDC.[271]

Project Hamilton's core objective was not to make policy decisions or recommendations but rather to develop and test experimental designs for a digital currency platform for the Federal Reserve. Specifically, it focused on transaction speeds and scalability, privacy, security, and resilience, among other things. It is unlikely that the Federal Reserve would participate in such a design project unless it believed there were a strong probability that a CBDC will be developed in the future.

Project Cedar, another CBDC initiative, was led by the Federal Reserve Bank of New York's Innovation Center. Unlike Project Hamilton, which focused on retail applications and was driven by the Boston Federal Reserve in partnership with MIT, Project Cedar focused on wholesale CBDC use cases, particularly in large-value interbank transactions and cross-border payments.[272]

Launched in 2021, Project Cedar was designed to explore how blockchain and distributed ledger technology could improve the speed, efficiency, and security of the foreign exchange settlement process, one of the most complex and time-sensitive components of the global financial system.[273]

The core goal of Project Cedar was to assess whether a CBDC platform could reduce the settlement risk inherent in current cross border payment systems, especially by enabling atomic settlement, a process in which two sides of a transaction are completed simultaneously or not at all, eliminating counterparty risk.

I'll again point out that it is unlikely that the Federal Reserve would be interested in Project Cedar if it weren't convinced that CBDCs are likely to be launched in the future, at least in some form.

I do want to clarify, though, that nothing I've presented thus far proves that American policymakers intend to impose a CBDC designed to restrict personal freedom, undermine consumer privacy, or advance ideological agendas. The fact that a CBDC could be used in such ways does not necessarily mean that it will be.

However, there is other compelling evidence that suggests this outcome is not only possible but it might also be under serious consideration currently.

CBDCs AND THE AMERICAN PROGRESSIVE POLICY MACHINE

In the United States, some central bank officials, government agencies, and left-leaning think tanks have already begun to talk about how a CBDC would align with their goals.

During his first two years in office, a key priority for President Biden was CBDC exploration. Prior to his reelection campaign, Biden and his administration advanced the country closer to the adoption of a CBDC than any other president.

In March 2022, Biden issued an executive order requiring federal agencies to explore the use of a CBDC and issue reports about its potential purpose and design. The order directed various federal agencies to assess the potential benefits and risks of a U.S. CBDC and to report their findings.[274]

Following the executive order, the Office of Science and Technology Policy published a report in September 2022 evaluating the technical possibilities for a U.S. CBDC system. The report outlined the Biden administration's policy objectives for a CBDC, including expanding equitable access to the financial system.

The Biden administration's 2022 objectives document titled "Policy Objectives for a U.S. Central Bank Digital Currency System" explicitly linked digital currency exploration with climate change goals and financial inclusion. According to the Biden White House, a future U.S. CBDC must "advance financial inclusion and equity" and "should improve environmental performance relative to the traditional financial system."[275]

As I noted in a March 2022 article for Fox Business,

A "fact sheet" released by the White House about the executive order [EO] also stated that its EO will "Promote Equitable Access to Safe and Affordable Financial Services" and that the government's report about the development of a digital dollar must "include implications for economic growth" and "financial growth and inclusion."

A senior administrative official also told reporters that the White House has and will continue to "partner with all stakeholders — including industry, labor, consumer, and environmental groups, international allies and partners" when developing plans for a central bank digital currency.[276]

Pay particular attention to that last part of the above quote. If someone were designing a digital currency with fair-minded, nonpartisan economic and monetary considerations in mind, there would be no need for advice from lobbying organizations and special-interest groups.

It seems apparent, based on these and other statements, that the Biden administration planned to use a CBDC as a policy tool to promote an ideological agenda. If government can impose rules on the use of money based on ideology, I will say that that is the end of freedom in our country.

Politicians are rarely open about their goals when discussing the possibility of a CBDC in press conferences and press releases or on radio and television shows. Any ideological aims of CBDC proponents are typically hidden by words like *efficiency, modernization, fraud prevention,* and *public safety,* just as they are in China.

Those in support of a CBDC often argue that it would make organized criminal enterprises almost impossible to operate, since government could track digital and programmable money easily. That is indeed true. There is also, however, a trail of policy statements, reports, and pilot projects indicating a clear intent to use the technology to change money into a programmable instrument of social policy. Goals like these are frequently touted as compassionate or inclusive; however, the overall effect could be the insertion of politics into every financial decision.

Consider a hypothetical example: A new CBDC benefit program for economically vulnerable communities offers enhanced payments for "environmentally sustainable" purchases. A family in Detroit wants to use its CBDC funds to buy a used SUV to commute to work, but the purchase is flagged as noncompliant because the vehicle exceeds acceptable emissions thresholds. Meanwhile, buying an electric car qualifies for a 10 percent government-funded cashback bonus, one that's applied automatically upon the purchase of the vehicle. In this scenario, there's no law banning SUV purchases; the pressure to conform to a certain behavior is built into the financial system itself.

Here's another hypothetical scenario. The Fed classifies financial support for certain social causes, religious organizations, or political movements as "supporting harmful misinformation." It then programs CBDCs so that they cannot be sent to groups that are flagged by designated government agencies, banks, or nonprofits as purveyors of "misinformation," making it nearly impossible for these groups to survive. Because the Fed is not a government agency, courts might allow such a design feature to exist. Even if courts forbid the Fed from engaging in authoritarian actions such as these, a private bank could engage in a similar action, depending on how a CBDC is designed. If dollars are digitized and programmable, anything is possible.

There are only three ways that I can think of to avoid scenarios such as these: prevent the creation of a CBDC in the first place; have Congress pass a law that forbids governments and private banks from using a CBDC to control people's legal behavior; have the courts step in and protect individual liberty. The question is whether you think any of these would happen if we were in the middle of a large economic crash. (I certainly don't think any are likely.)

What makes a CBDC so dangerous is precisely what makes it appealing to ruling-class lawmakers, Democrat and Republican alike: a CBDC could make it possible to impose ideology without legislation. Banks could impose large-scale economic, social, and cultural changes to transform society by using monetary rules applied to a digital currency. It is possible that courts would prevent that from happening; there is, however, no guarantee that they would. Banks are not government institutions in the same way the Treasury or Department of Defense is.

SHOULD YOU TRUST THE FEDERAL RESERVE?

Supporters of a CBDC will often agree that yes, a CBDC shouldn't be politicized; if its control is put into the hands of the Federal Reserve, there's nothing to worry about. The Federal Reserve isn't a political institution, we're told, and thus we can trust that it will treat people fairly. Put another way, *CBDC advocates want us to trust the experts.*

The Federal Reserve tries very hard not to get involved in political disputes, and it has been quite reticent on the topic of whether a CBDC will be created and what that could mean for U.S. citizens. There is, however, one little-known incident that sheds light on what the Federal Reserve is thinking about the use of a programmable CBDC.

In an obscure 2021 Federal Reserve Q&A session open to the

144 THE NEXT BIG CRASH

public, David Andolfatto, a senior economist and vice president at
the St. Louis Fed, responded to a question from a concerned citizen.

"Can you assure us that these digital currencies won't ever be used
to tell us when, how, or where our money can be spent?" asked the
individual.

That's a fair question. If the Federal Reserve has no plans to
implement such control mechanisms, I'd expect the answer to be
immediate and emphatic: *Absolutely not. That's not our job, and it
never will be.*

Instead, Andolfatto replied, "In life one can't give absolute
assurances of anything."[277]

Wait. What?

If there's no intent to use a digital dollar for social engineering or
behavioral controls, why dodge the question? Andolfatto's initial non-
answer suggests that control over how Americans use their money is
at least being considered behind closed doors.

He then went on to say, "I think the caller [questioner] is
concerned about the potential of privacy that would be associated,
say, with a government sort of digital currency. This is an ongoing
debate that we have all the time about how much privacy is
desirable."

I found that statement incredible. Andolfatto said that, in so many
words, that the Federal Reserve is actively debating the extent to
which Americans should be allowed to retain financial privacy and
individual liberty. (From my point of view, that admission alone
should be front-page news, especially in the context of any discussion
of a CBDC.)

To be fair, Andolfatto did offer what was (presumably) meant as
reassurance. He concluded his reply to the question by saying,

Obviously, in the United States we value personal privacy a lot,
and we let our representatives in Congress know that. And by and

large it's respected along many dimensions.

But there's a bit of a trade-off here as well because we don't know, for example, what sort of entities might make use of these central bank digital currencies for nefarious purposes, say, to finance terrorist activities. We might want the government to monitor certain types of transactions as well. And we see this in the anti-money laundering laws and the KYC [know your customer] laws. So, there's a trade-off. One can't give assurances, but I think what we can be assured of is that Congress will respond to the electorate's concerns and this is kind of the best we can hope for.[278]

So, according to a top economist at the Federal Reserve, the best safeguard for privacy in a future with government-issued programmable money is—Congress?

This is the same legislative body composed of people who can't seem to get anything done. The same group that has voted to take away our freedoms in the past. The group that has routinely failed to pass budgets on time and has spent tens of trillions of dollars more than the government has taken in. Congress is one of the least trustworthy, most highly criticized institutions in America, yet this expert at the Federal Reserve thinks we should be fine with putting our fate in the hands of Congress. (I have a better idea. Let's avoid the crisis altogether by never developing a CBDC in the first place.)

Andolfatto's assurance could be comical if the stakes weren't so high. The possibility that the United States could give control of a programmable digital currency to bureaucrats, technocrats, or central bankers is no minor matter, even if they do have congressional oversight.

THE STABLECOIN TRAP

The federal government has yet to create a consumer-based CBDC project, and the Trump administration has repeatedly said that it opposes programmable Cbdcs. The current head of the Federal Reserve, Jerome Powell, has also claimed that he won't allow the Federal Reserve to develop a CBDC while he's in charge.[279] But Donald Trump won't be president forever; Powell's term ends in May 2026; and crises have a tendency to change the way policymakers behave. A CBDC is likely to occur in the next big crash, and if it doesn't, it will most likely be because a CBDC alternative is already in the works or fully implemented.

When most people think of digital currencies, CBDCs or cryptocurrencies such as Bitcoin are the first things that come to mind. But there's another kind of digital currency that could end up becoming more widely used in America than both Bitcoin and CBDCs: stablecoins.

Stablecoins are a unique class of cryptocurrency designed to offer price stability by linking their value to a reserve asset. Typically, this reserve is a national fiat currency like the U.S. dollar, although it can also be a commodity such as gold or, in some cases, even other cryptocurrencies. The purpose of stablecoins is to combine the technological benefits of digital currencies (speed, programmability, and global accessibility) with the steadiness and predictability of traditional money.

There are several different models for achieving this price stability. The most common is fiat-backed stablecoins. These are digital tokens fully backed by actual reserves of currency held in banks or other trusted institutions. For every stablecoin in circulation, there is (supposed to be) an equivalent amount of fiat currency, such as dollars, held in reserve. Examples of this model include USD Coin (USDC) and Tether, both of which are pegged to the U.S. dollar and widely used in digital finance.

Another category is crypto-backed stablecoins. These are secured by other cryptocurrencies rather than fiat money. Because the value of cryptocurrencies can fluctuate wildly, these stablecoins are often at risk of over-collateralization. That means the issuing protocol holds more value in crypto than the value of the stablecoins issued; this creates a buffer against volatility. Often, this type of stablecoin is backed by a mix of other popular crypto assets, for example, Ethereum.

A third and more experimental approach is algorithmic stablecoins. These coins aim to keep their value steady relative to a reference currency through automated software and smart contracts that adjust supply and demand. Instead of being backed by reserves, the system increases or decreases the number of coins in circulation to hold prices at a consistent level. Although promising in theory, algorithmic stablecoins have faced serious challenges in practice, and some have collapsed entirely when their mechanisms failed to handle market stress.

Stablecoins are becoming a crucial component of the evolving digital financial system. They are used not only for cryptocurrency trading and investment but also for remittances, online payments, and decentralized finance applications. However, as they grow in popularity and influence, significant questions have risen about regulation, transparency, and the potential for centralized control, especially when tied to powerful private institutions or sanctioned by government oversight.

Enter the GENIUS Act, bipartisan legislation signed into law in 2025, with significant backing from President Trump.[280] Supporters have marketed the legislation as a great advance in digital currency oversight: it will bring much-needed structure, they say, to the stablecoin market, and will reinforce the value of digital assets used by millions across the globe.

I see this, however, as a perilous path toward centralized monetary power. I fear that the law could function as a veiled mechanism for ushering in a government-aligned digital dollar, one with minimal privacy guarantees and immense potential for surveillance and control.

The Guiding and Establishing National Innovation for U.S. Stablecoins Act, or the GENIUS Act, was created to legitimize stablecoins tied to the U.S. dollar, like USDC and Tether, which already account for more than $200 billion in circulation.[281] The legislation empowers stablecoin providers to operate under government oversight, lending institutional credibility to the technology. It mandates full transparency about reserve assets, routine public audits, and compliance with the Bank Secrecy Act, including know-your-customer and anti-money-laundering regulations.

Most important, the act insists that all issued stablecoins be backed 1:1 by highly liquid assets like U.S. dollars or Treasury bills. For every digital dollar circulating, there must be a matching dollar (or its Treasury equivalent) sitting in reserve. This is designed to reassure users that their tokens are always redeemable for traditional currency.[282]

These measures earned the GENIUS Act considerable praise in Congress, among members of both major political parties. However, while some aspects of the bill promote transparency, others lay the foundation for something dangerous. The GENIUS Act ties stablecoins to the authority of the U.S. government and forces compliance with strict federal mandates, which has positioned these currencies to become digital stand-ins for cash. In effect, it gives these assets the green light to function like official U.S. currency in most situations, only they're not managed directly by the Federal Reserve or the U.S. government, and their use isn't bound by constitutional safeguards.

That wouldn't be so concerning if there were strong consumer protections in place, but the GENIUS Act doesn't have privacy protections or safeguards to prevent discriminatory programming. That means stablecoins could easily become tools of ideological enforcement, not by an authoritarian government but by a massive corporation working hand in hand with government.

Imagine a future where stablecoins are widely used and are an integral part of the financial system. You attempt to contribute, using your stablecoins, to a controversial political cause, only to be blocked by the stablecoin issuer. You try to buy a nonelectric vehicle, red meat, or anything that falls afoul of an issuer's ESG criteria, so the system simply denies the transaction. Without guardrails, stablecoins could be programmed to restrict legal behavior based on arbitrary rules set by unelected corporations.

This may sound hard to believe, but there's nothing stopping this hypothetical future from becoming a reality, now that the federal government is putting its stamp of approval on many of the world's biggest stablecoins linked to the U.S. dollar.

The economic incentives for adopting these digital currencies are powerful. Compared to traditional dollars, stablecoins offer clear advantages: they can be transferred nearly instantly, incur virtually no transaction costs, and operate around the clock without relying on banking hours. They're affordable to issue, efficient to use, and globally accessible.

Now that Washington is certifying safety and reliability of stablecoins, their popularity is likely to surge, and with that surge will come the diminishing role of physical cash. As more institutions favor digital over traditional currency, Americans who wish to avoid programmable money may eventually find they have no viable alternative. Even if the traditional cash system is maintained officially, that will most likely not be widely used much longer when alternatives that appear significantly better exist, alternatives that are being tightly regulated by the federal government.

It might be easy to wonder why lawmakers were so enthusiastic to pass the GENIUS Act without any protections for individual rights and guards against social credit scores. I would say that you need to follow the money. The federal government is weighed down by an incredible amount of debt, and stablecoins could become the large new market needed to finance that debt.

The GENIUS Act demands that stablecoins be backed by either cash or Treasuries, and because Treasuries yield interest, they're the obvious choice for issuers. This creates a direct benefit for a federal government drowning in debt: When the government needs to finance its debt, it issues Treasury bonds, essentially IOUs from the government, and investors buy them with a promise that they will someday get their money back, plus interest.

Of course, investors around the world are increasingly more concerned about buying Treasury bonds themselves. The more reckless our government has become, the less interest investors have in financing America's debt. This has been evident during the country's recent inflation crisis: investors do not trust that the federal government can continue to finance its debt at the current staggering rate; better investment options are available, so there's no motivation to buy Treasury bonds.

The GENIUS Act, however, has helped to make Treasury bonds desirable again by requiring stablecoin issuers to hold cash or Treasury bonds. Regardless of whether bonds are a good investment, as stablecoins become more popular, there is a greater demand for Treasury bonds. From the government's perspective, increasing the legitimacy of stablecoins is a winning proposition.

The Treasury Department estimates that with legislation like the GENIUS Act in place, stablecoin reserves could absorb as much as $1 trillion in government debt by 2028. According to projections by Citibank, stablecoin issuers could accumulate as much as $1.2 trillion in U.S. Treasury securities by 2030.[283] The GENIUS Act is as much a financial rescue operation as it is a law-regulating technology.

There is a set of powerful interests lining up behind the GENIUS Act. Some major financial institutions are positioning themselves as central players in the stablecoin landscape, purchasing large stakes in top stablecoin ventures. Key examples are BlackRock and Fidelity, which have many connections to the World Economic Forum (WEF) and have agendas aligned with the ESG investing principle.[284] (ESG is a key focus of the Great Reset.) These organizations have a track record of using capital to advance political and social goals.

Let's look at BlackRock, one of the world's largest stockholders. It has a documented history of supporting progressive initiatives, particularly in the realms of environmental sustainability, social equity, and corporate governance. BlackRock CEO Larry Fink previously served on the board of trustees at the WEF and was a longtime ally of Klaus Schwab. Fink has played a pivotal role in pushing companies into adopting left-wing causes, such as climate change and energy use. He and BlackRock have likely done more to promote the Great Reset and ESG than any other private entity.[285]

If BlackRock and other Great Reset institutions and individuals gain control over the infrastructure of digital finance, they could shape economic behavior with an unprecedented level of precision and authority. I'm not sure that these are the entities who should be determining what we can and cannot do with our own money; they are certainly not gatekeepers I would trust to protect civil liberties.

Americans who value the preservation of liberty, at least as it has been understood in the United States, should see the GENIUS Act as a wake-up call. Unless we require lawmakers to revise the law regulating stablecoins to include clear protections for individual rights, we will walk blindly into an era in which every transaction is monitored, every dollar traceable, and every act of dissent punishable through economic coercion.

THE ROAD AHEAD: WHAT A U.S. CBDC MIGHT LOOK LIKE AFTER THE CRASH

The next big financial crisis might be a moment of rapid reordering. Think back to the 2008 crisis, which ushered in an era of bailouts, central bank interventions, and massive money printing. In a similar way, the next crash could normalize state-issued programmable money as a response to widespread hardship, and once the infrastructure is in place, the door is open to misuse and abuse.

In the best-case scenario, a CBDC is rolled out with built-in protections: private wallets, minimal surveillance, and no ideological programming. It coexists with physical cash and is used as a convenience, not a mandate. (That is, in my opinion, unlikely.)

In a more realistic scenario, once a CBDC is implemented, it will eventually become mandatory for receiving certain kinds of government aid or participating in key sectors of the economy. Based on how major changes like this have happened in history, it will be voluntary at first. Then, over time, incentives like faster payments, tax rebates, or emergency relief funds will nudge more people into the system. As adoption grows, so will the conditions attached. Use the CBDC for certain green purchases? Earn a rebate. Try to use it to buy ammo or make a political donation to the "wrong" candidate? Get flagged. Slowly, the CBDC transitions from money into a tool of social engineering.

Consider another hypothetical but entirely plausible scenario. John Miller is a small business owner in rural Ohio. An economic crash in 2028 leads to his customers dwindling, his business drying up, and his bank restricting access to his capital. In response, Congress passes a law authorizing a new CBDC, which is managed by both the Federal Reserve and private banks. The Federal Reserve then launches a stimulus program offering every citizen $1,200 worth of a new digital currency. All John has to do to receive it is to download a CBDC wallet approved by the Federal Reserve and managed by a private banking institution.

He signs up reluctantly, and at first, it is a lifeline. He uses the funds to buy groceries and pay for utilities. However, when he places an online ammunition order for his family's long-time hunting tradition, his bank denies the transaction. The app informs him, "Transaction blocked—high-risk item."

A week later, he donates $100 to a political action committee opposing new climate legislation. The next morning, his wallet displays a warning: "Unusual political contribution detected. CBDC privileges under review."

During a trip across state lines to visit a relative, his fuel purchases are flagged as exceeding his monthly carbon allotment. The app denies further gas station transactions until the next cycle.

The steps described above seem like reasonable measures to fight extremism, climate change, or gun violence, but it is actually financial control disguised as public safety.

This concept is already being debated in mainstream political discourse. Florida Governor Ron DeSantis signed legislation in 2023 that banned the use of any federal CBDC in his state, calling it a "surveillance tool" and warning that it could be used to enforce ESG scores on citizens. (Whether such a ban would hold up in court, however, is uncertain.)[286]

In 2024 and again in 2025, congressman Tom Emmer (R-MN) introduced the CBDC Anti-Surveillance State Act. The legislation seeks to stop the Federal Reserve from issuing a direct-to-consumer CBDC without explicit congressional approval and to block the federal government from creating or using a digital dollar in a way that could lead to mass surveillance, loss of financial privacy, or centralized control over personal transactions. At the time of publication of this book, it has not yet been passed and made into law.[287]

These two examples reflect a growing awareness on the political right of the risks posed by programmable state money. I am concerned, however, that many Americans may not see those risks until after a time of desperation comes. By that point, it will be too late. People who are hungry, broke, or desperate to keep a business afloat may find the offer of fast, free money through a government app too tempting to resist. (This is why crises are so often launching pads for policies that may not succeed in times of stability.)

The real danger is not a CBDC; it's the infrastructure and mindset that comes with it. A system in which a user's financial behavior can be monitored, rated, or restricted based on a carbon footprint, public statements, or social views is incompatible with the American concept of liberty. However, that's exactly the kind of system that could emerge with the next big crash.

WHAT RESISTANCE COULD LOOK LIKE

After all this bad news, I must tell you the good news: Americans are not powerless to prevent the deployment of a CBDC. Yes, it's a technological innovation that seems unlikely to go away anytime soon, but its large-scale implementation will be a political decision. And political decisions can be challenged at the state level, through litigation, and by public dissent.

Several states have already begun erecting legal firewalls to guard against a federal CBDC. In addition to Florida, states like Alabama, Indiana, South Dakota, and Nebraska have introduced or passed legislation that would reject a CBDC as legal tender or prohibit its use in certain contexts. These efforts may appear to be mainly symbolic, but they do form a foundation for coordinated pushback against a federal CBDC that could block its adoption nationwide.[288, 289]

Litigation will also play a role. Legal challenges on First and Fourth Amendment grounds are inevitable if a CBDC has ideological conditions, such as purchase restrictions based on environmental impact or political affiliations. Lawsuits over compelled speech, political discrimination, or unreasonable search and seizure could tie up implementation for years, especially if the Supreme Court weighs in.

Another defense against the dangers of a CBDC must come from civil society. Americans must understand that their individual liberty is at stake. Pro-liberty think tanks, talk radio and television shows, constitutional law centers, and grassroots organizations will need to inform and mobilize the public.

Americans can also take advantage of opportunities to champion CBDC alternatives: the use of physical cash, private cryptocurrencies, or non-CBDC digital payment systems can serve as both a protest and a practical hedge. The preservation of financial freedom may depend on building robust alternatives that render it unnecessary. (Stablecoins are actually a good example of a potentially good alternative to a CBDC. Had the GENIUS Act protected individual rights, it could have provided an excellent alternative to CBDCs.)

If the future of money is indeed digital, then the fight must be to ensure that digital money remains decentralized, private, and resistant to ideological interference. The outcome of that battle will depend on how seriously Americans take the warnings and how prepared they are to act when the next crash opens the door to change.

CONCLUSION: A WARNING AND A CALL TO ACTION

The prospect of a central bank digital currency may sound abstract to many Americans today—a distant, technocratic policy debate by institutions far removed from daily life. I would sound a word of caution here: as history has shown us, crises can turn abstract debates into mandates. What seems improbable in times of stability can

156 THE NEXT BIG CRASH

become policy in moments of chaos.

The next major economic crash will likely bring about just such a moment in the United States People reeling from financial loss and institutional failure will look for rapid solutions. Among the proposals on the table, a CBDC will likely be presented as offering secure money, immediate aid, and economic stability. The fine print, of course, may likely be buried under the promises.

For Americans who want to preserve the liberties we have, the time to resist is before the crisis hits. Educate your community. Support state-level legislation to block CBDC mandates. Demand transparency from federal institutions and protections for individual rights in stablecoins and other emerging technologies. Insist that Congress, rather than central banks or unelected bureaucrats, make decisions about the future of our money. Perhaps most important, in my opinion, support alternative means of payment that keep money out of the hands of those who wish to use it to enforce ideology.

Financial liberty and personal liberty are inseparable. If the government can control how you earn, save, and spend your money, it can control other aspects of your life. It can punish dissent, reward conformity, and enforce compliance with the values of whoever is in charge. (This is why the Chinese Communist Party is such a big fan of CBDCs.)

If the digital dollar is implemented in the way many elites envision, neutral money would come to an end in America. It would be the beginning of programmable currency and, with it, programmable behavior.

The story, however, has not been written yet. Vigilance, courage, and action are key. We can choose a different path.

In the months and years to come, we may be told that CBDCs are inevitable. That they're efficient, modern, and progressive. That we must adopt them to remain competitive on the global stage. I must point out, though, that inevitability is a myth.

Every policy is a choice. Every architecture is a decision. Every American, whether in government, business, or the voting booth, has a role to play in shaping what comes next.

We must not shut our eyes and walk blindly into a future in which money becomes a tool of surveillance and compliance is the cost of participation. Once a system is in place, it will monitor our lives and redefine what freedom means and who gets to have it. We must speak now while it still matters. Act while we still can. Build while there's still time.

I realize that the subjects I have presented are difficult to absorb and most likely rather discouraging, but don't panic. In the next chapter, we'll turn our attention to practical steps you can take to protect yourself and your family. In my opinion, you can avoid many of the worst consequences by preparing wisely in advance. Preparation won't eliminate every risk, but it will put you in a far stronger position than most.

5

HOW TO PREPARE FOR THE NEXT BIG CRASH

When I first began researching the topics discussed in this book (securities ownership, Wall Street's hidden risks, the global push for central bank digital currencies, and the incredible scope of government emergency powers), I was stunned.

I've spent years studying financial systems, government policy, and the forces that shape global economics, but even I wasn't prepared for what I discovered. Each layer that I uncovered revealed a more unsettling reality. Our system is fragile, yes, but it's even worse than that. It is rigged. I realized that most Americans, even those who think they're well-informed, have no idea how exposed they are.

Initially, I didn't know what to do. The implications were overwhelming. I felt a deep sense of urgency, not just as a researcher or writer, but as a husband and father. How would I protect my family if the very foundation of our financial system were to collapse? What good are paper investments if the laws and institutions you trust to uphold them are designed to fail you when you need them most?

So, I got to work.

I spent months digging, consulting financial experts, attorneys, historians, economists, and former Wall Street insiders. I read legislation, combed through legal codes, spoke with lawmakers, and asked the hard questions that few others seemed willing to confront.

I am not a financial adviser, and I do not claim to have all the answers. Please consult a licensed professional before making any investment decisions of your own. With that said, I believe the knowledge I have gathered could make a meaningful difference for people who want to prepare themselves and their families for the challenges ahead.

In this final chapter, I will walk you through what I am doing to prepare and, more importantly, *why*. This is not a blueprint for every reader, and it is certainly not investment advice. It is a deeply personal account of how I have tried to make sense of a system teetering on the edge of disaster and how I have chosen to respond.

The following sections describe the principles that now guide my own approach to financial and personal preparedness. Each principle reflects lessons I have learned through research, experience, and long conversations with experts, family, and friends. My hope is that, as you read through these sections, you will find ideas worth adapting to your own circumstances, strategies that can spark your own thinking, and, most of all, the conviction that you do not have to wait for disaster to strike before taking action.

DIVERSIFICATION

One of the best pieces of advice my dad gave me is that diversification is the key to financial security. "You never put all your eggs in one basket," he told me. And he's right. The more I have learned about the financial system, the more obvious it is that you cannot trust any one part of it with all your wealth.

I diversify my wealth across many different kinds of assets: precious metals like gold, cryptocurrencies, cash, old books signed by famous people, art, and real estate. And yes, in case you are wondering, I do continue to invest in securities, despite the dangers discussed in chapter 2. Securities investments remain one of the best ways to build long-term wealth. But I would never rely on securities markets the way I once thought people should.

I don't know what the future is going to bring, and neither does anyone else. I believe the best way to protect yourself, no matter what happens, is to have spread your wealth across all types of assets.

ASSET CUSTODY AND OWNERSHIP

Equally as important as diversification is understanding how your assets are understood to be yours. As I explained in earlier chapters, the majority of Americans do not own their securities in the way they think they do. You may have bought shares of a stock or invested in a mutual fund, but in most cases, you are not the registered owner of those securities. Instead, you have a security entitlement, which is essentially a contractual relationship that gives you certain rights and benefits tied to the underlying asset. However, laws and regulations can change. You should not expect that the rights and benefits you have now will always be there, especially in the midst of a crisis.

I do not demand direct registration or physical custody of every investment I make. Doing so would be costly and impractical. I still hold securities in traditional brokerage accounts, as do many Americans, but I no longer assume that those assets are entirely safe or fully under my control. I have worked hard to understand the legal structure surrounding those holdings. And I have taken steps to reduce my exposure so that I'm not dependent on one broker or bank. If I cannot control the system, I can at least limit how much of my wealth is trapped in it and how many institutions are involved.

That is also why I have increasingly focused on tangible assets, things I can physically hold or control. You cannot confiscate a gold coin in the same way you can freeze a brokerage account. You cannot digitally erase land or a piece of art. In a world that is becoming more digitized, more centralized, and more fragile, physical assets offer peace of mind that no spreadsheet or online statement ever could.

As a general rule, I try to keep about 10 to 20 percent of my wealth invested in precious metals and other physical assets. Some people may consider having that much in tangible holdings is too risky because of the possibility of theft or loss. But there are plenty of financial institutions that offer secure, insured storage for a relatively low cost. For me, the benefits of holding real, untraceable assets far outweigh the risks.

STAYING LIQUID

No matter how well diversified your portfolio is, or how confident you feel in your long-term investments, there is one simple truth about financial preparedness that you should not ignore: if you cannot access your money when you need it, none of it matters. In a crisis, liquidity is essential.

During the early days of the COVID-19 pandemic, we saw what can happen when financial systems are under strain. Banks reduced hours or closed entirely.[290] In some locations, ATMs ran out of cash. Tens of millions of Americans lost their jobs, overwhelming state unemployment systems, which had to delay unemployment benefits and leave many people without income for weeks or even months.[291] Imagine that scenario happening on a much larger scale, with a systemic crisis underway. Would you be able to buy food, fuel, medicine, or other necessities if your accounts were suddenly locked or emptied?

This is why I have made it a personal priority to keep a portion of my wealth in liquid, accessible forms. That includes physical cash stored securely in multiple locations, precious metals in denominations small enough to be practical in a pinch, and digital assets held in private wallets instead of centralized exchanges. I do not keep all of it in one place or under one roof. If one channel is compromised, others are still available.

Liquidity gives you options. It allows you to act quickly if a unique opportunity presents itself or if your family faces an unexpected need. It protects you from the panic that sets in when systems go down and millions of people realize, all at once, that they cannot access their money. It gives you the power to say no to offers or mandates that you may otherwise feel that you have to accept, simply because you need a lifeline.

INVESTING IN SKILLS AND PEOPLE

When most people think about protecting their wealth, they think about money. They think about accounts, portfolios, interest rates, and inflation. And those things do matter. But over time, I have come to realize that real preparedness is about much more than financial instruments. It is about what you know and what you can do, especially when systems fail.

One of the most overlooked forms of wealth is practical skill. In a crisis, the people who know how to fix things, grow food, source clean water, or build relationships will be far better off than those who have never had to solve a problem without a phone or a financial adviser. That's why, in addition to investing in hard assets, my wife and I also invest in the ability to live more independently, solve problems creatively, and help others when it counts.

That does not mean that I have gone off the grid or built a bunker in the woods. It does mean that I've started to think more seriously about the kinds of skills that might matter most in the future. I have taken steps to learn basic home repair. I've begun experimenting with small-scale gardening. I've studied how people prepare for power outages, food shortages, and financial disruptions—not because I expect the worst to happen tomorrow but because I refuse to be caught off guard.

Self-defense is another area I take seriously. In times of chaos or economic collapse, law enforcement resources can become strained or unavailable. You cannot assume someone else will protect your home or your loved ones. I have invested time and resources into making sure my family and I are capable of defending ourselves, if necessary. That includes training in the legal and responsible use of firearms and clear communication with those closest to me about how we would respond in an emergency. I hope I never need to use any of it, but I would rather be prepared than not.

Most importantly, I've involved my family in this process. I want my children to grow up understanding how the world works, how fragile our systems really are, and how important it is to be capable and resilient. I want them to know what it means to solve real problems, not just outsource them.

Community matters too. One of the smartest decisions I've made is to live close to family and friends, the people I trust and know I can rely on if things get hard. No one can prepare for every possible scenario alone. We were designed to live in community, not isolation. I've also found that joining a church or other values-based organizations can make all the difference. When trouble comes, it's not the government or your social media followers who will show up at your door. It's your pastor, your neighbor, your brother, your sister, or your best friend. Build those relationships now. They will be your most valuable asset later.

Another factor I now take seriously is geography. I believe it is incredibly important to live in or near communities with active farms and food producers. You can have all the money in the world, but if the grocery store shelves are empty and the supply chains are broken, you will need local options. Stable, nearby sources of food are a foundational part of preparedness. Being close to agricultural communities—people who know how to grow, raise, and distribute food—gives you a huge advantage when national systems falter.

Now, I want to be honest with you. I am not naturally good at a lot of these things. I grew up in a family in which practical skills like gardening, fixing engines, and building things from scratch were a regular part of life. My dad knew how to do just about everything, but when I was younger, I wasn't interested in learning. I was focused on other things, and I didn't see the value of those skills at the time.

That is exactly why I decided to start learning later in life. You do not need to be an expert or grow up with a survivalist mindset to make progress. You just need to recognize the risks and take the first steps. I'm hardly an expert at home improvement, but I have become dramatically better in that department, and I'm fortunate to have people around me who are far more capable in these areas.

My wife is much more skilled than I am when it comes to gardening, food preservation, and sustainability, for example. My father is more experienced with firearms, defensive preparedness, and construction and home improvement. I have learned a great deal just by asking questions and being willing to admit what I do not know. That is the key: build relationships with people you trust and start developing the skills that you can reasonably manage. You don't have to do everything, but you do need to do *something*.

This kind of preparation is not about fear. It is about freedom. When you have real skills, you are harder to control. You are less dependent on fragile systems. And you are in a much better position to help your community instead of becoming another person in need of rescue.

If the next big crash does arrive, there is a good chance that traditional institutions will struggle to respond quickly or effectively. There is also the possibility, as I've shown throughout this book, that they will use the crisis as an opportunity to limit your freedom and make you more dependent on government. That is when knowledge becomes power. That is when people who can repair, grow, build, or organize will become the backbone of local resilience.

In the years ahead, financial strategies will still matter, but they will not be enough on their own. Every American who wants to protect their family and preserve their freedom should be thinking about more than money. They should be building the kinds of skills that cannot be stolen, frozen, or inflated away.

MY INVESTMENT PORTFOLIO

Throughout this chapter, I have outlined the principles and values that guide how I prepare for the next big crash. But I know many readers are wondering, "What are you actually doing with your money?" In this section, I want to give you a clear picture of my personal investment strategy, not because I think it's the perfect model for everyone but because I believe in being transparent about what I'm doing and why.

Before I go any further, let me reiterate what I said earlier in the chapter: I am not a financial adviser. Nothing in this chapter (or anywhere in this book) should be interpreted as investment advice. Every person's financial situation is different, and you should always consult a licensed professional before making decisions about your portfolio.

With that said, here's how I'm currently allocating my wealth (excluding the equity I hold in my home).

I keep about 10 to 20 percent of my assets in precious metals like gold and silver. I like that these assets are tangible, portable, and free from digital oversight. They are not dependent on an internet connection, an exchange platform, or a government guarantee. They have been used as money for thousands of years, and I believe they will continue to hold value in times of crisis. This portion of my portfolio gives me peace of mind and a degree of independence that other assets cannot provide.

I keep another 10 to 20 percent in cryptocurrencies, depending on what's happening in the market. I believe crypto has enormous long-term potential, especially as a hedge against central bank digital currencies and runaway monetary policy. I do not treat crypto as a get-rich-quick scheme, and I do not chase hype. I focus on long-term projects and technologies that I believe have staying power. I also take custody seriously. I never leave large balances on centralized exchanges, and I use private wallets to ensure I retain as much control as possible.

I usually invest about 30 to 40 percent of my assets in a heavily diversified stock portfolio. (I say "usually" because, at present, I'm more concerned than usual about a stock market crash, so I've recently sold many of my securities.) My portfolio typically includes more than a hundred companies. I do not rely on a handful of tech giants or put all of my trust in one sector. I spread out my risk, monitor my holdings, and adjust when necessary. I still believe that equity markets have value, especially in the long run, but only if they are balanced by other types of assets.

The remaining portion of my wealth is split between multiple checking, savings, money-market, and certificate of deposit (CD) accounts at different financial institutions. (CD accounts provide a much better return than checking and savings accounts.) I do not ever want my cash to be all in one place. I do this for both practical and strategic reasons. From a practical perspective, if a single bank experiences trouble or a temporary freeze, I may lose access to some of my funds but not to all. Strategically speaking, I view these different accounts not as investment vehicles but as tools for stability and liquidity.

This is not a flashy strategy. It's not designed to maximize returns in any one year. It's meant for durability and flexibility in a future filled with uncertainty and political risk. I want to be ready for a wide range of scenarios, and that means building a portfolio that is broad, balanced, and resilient.

LEGISLATIVE SOLUTIONS

There are also some important legislative changes that could be made to help protect people. They will happen, however, only if millions of Americans stand up and demand greater legal protections. Many politicians are motivated by a desire to remain in office, and they gauge how well they are doing in that department in large part by how their constituents communicate with them.

I have spoken with countless Americans who believe that telling lawmakers about their concerns accomplishes nothing, but that couldn't be further from the truth. I know many lawmakers. I've worked with them. I have been involved in numerous legislative fights at the state level, all across the country. And I can tell you with confidence that lawmakers absolutely care about what their constituents are fired up about—but the only way for them to know that will be for people to express their views clearly and politely.

The following policy reforms would go a long way toward protecting individuals from the threats described in this book. I hope you'll take the time to consider them and perhaps even share these ideas with your state legislators.

Revising the Uniform Commercial Code

In chapter 2, I explained the reality of owning securities for most Americans: how most individuals and institutions do not have full control or ownership of their securities investments (like stocks and bonds) but rather possess securities entitlements, which are essentially contracts that grant certain rights and benefits to investors (not direct, registered ownership of securities). The rights outlined in securities entitlements can be altered by changes in laws and regulations, which can weaken or eliminate protections for consumers who hold securities entitlements. That is exactly what has occurred.

As noted in chapter 2, the Uniform Commercial Code (a state law enacted by all fifty states) has now been amended so that, if a large Wall Street firm collapses, financial institutions are given priority over securities used as collateral. This means that if a failing broker has improperly used its customers' stocks, bonds, or other securities as collateral in a lending agreement, the lender might be able to seize customers' investments to cover its losses, even though the customers did nothing wrong.[292]

Even more concerning is the possibility that, during a major financial crash, lawmakers could change laws and regulations that are supposed to prevent Wall Street firms from using customers' assets as collateral. Changes like these could potentially open the floodgates to reckless lending practices that could put your wealth at risk.[293]

The best way to resolve the problems described in chapter 2 is to completely restructure Wall Street's current way of operating, restoring investors' direct control over securities for the first time in a half century. Unfortunately, returning to a paper-based, decentralized securities system is highly impractical and unadvisable. Wall Street is now entirely dependent on the current, centralized model of securities ownership managed by the Depository Trust Company (DTC). If states or the federal government were to return direct, registered ownership of securities to individuals tomorrow, the existing system would likely collapse.

Perhaps a gradual transition to a digital, tokenized securities-ownership model could be achieved. "Tokenized securities are when the ownership of a security is materialized through the issuance of a token that is registered on a distributed ledger technology (DLT) infrastructure of blockchain."[294] Put simply, a tokenized security is sort of like a cryptocurrency that's tied to a security investment, such as a stock or bond. Blockchain technology makes it possible for an individual to directly own a security and easily transfer it to another party on an exchange without the need for the vast financial infrastructure required under the current DTC-centered model.

The idea of tokenized securities is promising, but it would take many years for such a system to develop, and the regulatory, legal, and institutional hurdles that would need to be cleared for widespread adoption would be immense.

A more realistic short-term solution is for state lawmakers to amend the Uniform Commercial Code so that it explicitly prioritizes individual investors over secured creditors in bankruptcy proceedings involving financial intermediaries. Put simply, states should revise the current law so that, if a Wall Street firm goes bankrupt, investors recover their money before big financial institutions, regardless of the specific circumstances. This straightforward change to Article 8 of the Uniform Commercial Code would strengthen confidence in the system without dismantling its core framework.

Critics of this approach have argued that implementing such changes would create complications for customers' margin accounts. A margin account is a type of brokerage account that allows you to borrow money from your broker to purchase investments, such as stocks. It is similar to taking out a loan. You contribute your own funds for part of the investment, and the broker lends you the remainder. This enables you to buy more than you could with just your own money, which can increase potential gains but also heightens the risk of greater losses.

Here is a simple way to understand it: If you have $1,000 and open a margin account, your broker might allow you to borrow another $1,000. Now you can buy $2,000 worth of stocks. If the stock rises, you earn more than you would have otherwise. But if the stock falls, you could lose more, and you are still responsible for repaying the borrowed amount, together with interest.

Customers who use margin accounts receive special benefits (namely, access to additional capital), by permitting their securities to be used as collateral and, in some cases, allowing brokers to lend out or rehypothecate those assets. (Rehypothecation is when a broker or other financial institution uses the collateral it received from a client as its own collateral in another transaction.)

To preserve the use of margin accounts, lawmakers would need to build exceptions into the law for this special arrangement, as well as for other exceptions. These exceptions, however, should not prevent policymakers from protecting the tens of millions of Americans who do not use margin accounts.

State legislatures should also launch broader reviews of their commercial codes to identify and fix other vulnerabilities that could be exploited during a crisis. The time to do this is *now*, before another collapse puts Americans' life savings in jeopardy. Investors deserve clear rules, strong protections, and a system that works for them, not just for those who helped to create the system.

If all this Wall Street jargon has your head spinning, don't worry. All you need to know is that states can and should amend the Uniform Commercial Code to better protect individual investors in the event of a major crash. There are plenty of experts for lawmakers to consult on this issue, including the Pro-Family Legislative Network (PFLN). PFLN's experts have been working for the past few years to persuade lawmakers to make these and other commonsense reforms.[295] In order for groups like PFLN to be successful, though, more public pressure is needed. Without it, I fear the problem will never be solved, at least not without a great deal of pain and suffering.

Transactional Gold

As I discussed in chapter 4, a U.S. central bank digital currency (CBDC) could be used by government or the Federal Reserve to severely limit people's freedoms and privacy. Depending on a CBDC's design, it could control what people spend their money on and could be used to track individuals' behavior. CBDCs would also make it easier for the federal government and the Federal Reserve to create more currency. This is, in my opinion, a truly terrifying possibility, considering how very unwise both institutions have been in recent years with spending and monetary policy.

Here's the big problem for state lawmakers seeking to protect their citizens from a future programmable CBDC: the federal government has the exclusive authority under the U.S. Constitution to regulate money. In Article I, Section 8, Clause 5 of the Constitution, Congress is given the power to "coin Money, regulate the Value thereof, and of foreign Coin, and fix the Standard of Weights and Measures." That means if Congress were to create a CBDC or empower the Federal Reserve or private banks to do it, states could do very little to stop them.

However, while states cannot block Congress from creating a CBDC, they do have some power to mitigate the misuse of a CBDC. That's where something called transactional gold comes in. Transactional gold is a proposal for states to recognize gold as legal tender and to create the infrastructure needed for consumers to conduct transactions quickly and efficiently using gold or other precious metals.[296]

In practice, transactional gold would rely on a system that digitizes ownership of gold held in secure, state-regulated vaults. Customers could deposit physical gold or purchase gold from a state-affiliated institution. That gold would then be held in their name and made spendable using a digital payment platform, similar to how a debit card works with a traditional bank account.

Imagine a state-backed app or card linked to your gold holdings. When you buy a cup of coffee, you swipe your card or scan your phone, and the system instantly converts a tiny portion of your gold into dollars for the merchant or, better yet, transfers the gold itself to the merchant, if the merchant accepts gold-backed payments directly. The exchange could happen in real time at the point of sale, using market prices to determine value.

One of the earliest and most important intellectual leaders of the transactional gold movement has been Kevin Freeman, a financial expert and national security analyst who has long warned about the dangers of a digital-only currency system.[297] Freeman has worked for years to educate lawmakers, especially at the state level, about how transactional gold could serve as both a check against centralized monetary control and a safeguard for economic freedom. His leadership has been instrumental in advancing gold-as-money legislation in states like Texas and Florida, laying the groundwork for the kinds of systems now being proposed across the country.

The movement is gaining real momentum. As of mid-2025, more than a dozen states have introduced or passed legislation that recognizes gold and silver as legal tender or supports the creation of transactional gold systems. Texas has established a state-run gold depository and has approved transactional gold.[298] Florida, Louisiana, and Utah have also taken significant steps toward establishing transactional gold.[299] These efforts represent the beginning of a nationwide pushback against the looming threat of a CBDC and fiat dependency. States do, indeed, have tools to fight back.

It would be crucial for a transactional gold system to be built outside the Federal Reserve system. If implemented correctly, it would give citizens an off-ramp from the collapsing fiat currency regime and a refuge from the surveillance and control mechanisms built into CBDCs. Your wealth wouldn't sit in a politically manipulated bank account. It would be held in real, tangible assets that have preserved value for thousands of years. Transactional gold systems would make those assets just as spendable as the dollars in your pocket and not under the control of Washington's technocrats.

Of course, for transactional gold to scale effectively, more states would need to repeal legal tender laws that penalize or exclude gold in commerce. They would need to build robust digital infrastructure and possibly partner with private companies already working on gold-backed payment solutions. The key point, though, is that transactional gold allows states to offer their citizens a very real means of escape from a financial future dominated by CBDCs.

Balanced Budget Amendment

One of the longest-running attempts to shore up the dollar, avoid a CBDC, and usher in a new era of fiscal responsibility is the movement to create a balanced budget amendment (BBA). A BBA would not stop Congress from creating a programmable CBDC that could be used to control people's behavior or destroy privacy, but it would make a CBDC less desirable by strengthening the current monetary system. More importantly, even if a CBDC were created, a BBA would blunt its economic impact because a BBA requirement would, in effect, put strict limits on how much money could be created by the federal government. That would make it difficult or impossible for a future federal government to print hundreds of billions or even trillions of new digital dollars with the push of a button.

For decades, lawmakers and activists have been demanding an amendment to the U.S. Constitution that would require Congress and the president to spend responsibly. However, Congress has shown very little interest in pursuing it since the amendment would, by design, limit federal power.

Thankfully, Article V of the Constitution provides two ways to create amendments, and one of them doesn't require the consent of Congress. The first and most popular method for amending the Constitution is for Congress to propose and approve amendments. Under this pathway, two-thirds of both the House of Representatives and the Senate must pass a proposed amendment before it can move to the next step. The second way to amend the Constitution is for two-thirds of state legislatures to call for an amendments convention, which allows states to pass their own amendments without the approval of Congress.[300]

In both cases, "A proposed amendment becomes part of the Constitution as soon as it is ratified by three-fourths of the States (38 of 50 States)."[301] Without ratification from three quarters of the states, a proposed amendment cannot become law, regardless of whether the majority of members of Congress voted in favor of it.

Although there are two ways to amend the Constitution, "None of the 27 amendments to the Constitution have been proposed by constitutional convention."[302] All of them have originated in Congress. However, there is currently a growing number of activists, scholars, and legislators who are trying to change that.

Congress and presidents appear to have no intention of fixing America's spending problem. The value of the traditional dollar is being destroyed, making it much more likely that a new currency will have to replace it someday. Among the options available, a CBDC is by far the leading option for lawmakers and central banks. States need to take matters into their own hands by calling for an Article V amendments convention for the purpose of passing a BBA to the

U.S. Constitution. Ideally, states could go one step further by also creating a constitutional amendment that forever bans the use of a programmable digital currency by the Federal Reserve or the federal government.

Although the BBA movement does not get a lot of attention in the press, it has gained significant momentum in recent years. Twenty-seven states have passed Article V resolutions specifically calling for a BBA convention.[303] Only thirty-four states are needed to create the convention that would draft the BBA. (The three-fourths requirement for state ratification would still need to be met after the amendment is approved.)

A related but distinct effort called the Convention of States is working to get states to call for a convention to draft amendments that would "limit the power and jurisdiction of the federal government, impose fiscal restraints, and place term limits on federal officials." At present, nineteen states have passed the Convention of States proposal, including Arizona, Utah, Wisconsin, and Texas.[304]

The effort to pass a new balanced-budget amendment is far from over, but considering how important and far-reaching a BBA would be, it's remarkable how close states have come to reaching the threshold required to call for an Article V amendments convention. I fear, though, that the worse America's debt crisis becomes, the harder it's going to be to get the amendment over the finish line. That might seem counterintuitive, but if you consider it for a moment, it makes perfect sense. State legislatures are becoming increasingly more dependent on federal debt spending. At some point, it seems plausible that many lawmakers who might otherwise be in favor of a BBA will believe the federal dollars are too important to lose, killing any hope of a BBA. The process is a worthy one, but it might be moving too slowly to stop the next big crash or the implementation of a CBDC system in America.

CONCLUSION

If you've made it this far in the book, I want to thank you, not just for reading but for caring. Most people will never ask the questions explored in these pages. Most will never take the time to understand how the modern financial system actually works, how fragile it has become, and how much power has been consolidated into the hands of unelected elites and centralized institutions. You have. And that matters.

The next big crash may not look like the last one. It might not begin on Wall Street or start with a housing collapse. It could be sparked by a geopolitical conflict, a cyberattack, a pandemic, a natural disaster, or something else that we cannot imagine. No matter how the crisis begins, however, its effects will be felt by every household, every business, and every institution in America. No one will be fully immune.

The choice we all face is simple: prepare, or don't.

Some will cling to the hope that politicians, regulators, or central banks will fix the problems in time. That's not a bet I'm willing to make. The record of the past two decades, especially during the COVID-19 crisis, has made it painfully clear that those in power are far more interested in expanding their control than in protecting your freedom or financial well-being.

Others will retreat into denial, believing that nothing that serious could ever happen in America. History tells a different story. Financial collapse is a recurring feature of centralized, overleveraged systems. Once the cracks form, they widen fast. That's why this book was never just about sounding the alarm; it is about providing a path forward.

You now understand how vulnerable our system is. You know how your securities are held, who really owns what, and what might happen if the laws change under stress. You know that CBDCs aren't a distant hypothetical. They are already being tested and quietly built. You know that in times of crisis, governments use "emergency powers" not to free people but to control them.

But you also know that you have options. You can diversify. You can take custody of more of your assets. You can invest in skills, people, and local communities. You can push your state lawmakers to reform the laws that endanger your wealth and your liberty. And you can work to build a future in which real money, constitutional limits, and decentralized power once again define the American system.

The truth is that no single person can stop the next big crash. The forces driving us toward the edge are bigger than any one of us. But that doesn't mean we are helpless. Every family that prepares becomes one more family that is not dependent on government. Every state that resists centralized currency schemes makes it harder for federal elites to impose them. Every person who learns how the system really works becomes a voice for truth in a sea of confusion and propaganda.

You don't need to predict the exact timing of the crash to prepare for it. You just need to recognize that the risks are real and that the system is not nearly as stable, secure, or trustworthy as you've been led to believe.

When the dust settles, the people who endure will not be the ones with the most money in digital bank accounts. They'll be the ones who saw the storm coming and took action. They'll be the ones who invested in real value, real skills, and real relationships. They'll be the ones who refused to be controlled. You still have time to be one of those people, but that window is closing.

Prepare, learn, and act now. Once the next big crash begins, it won't be a warning. It will be too late.

ENDNOTES

1   Hiranmayi Srinivasan, "U.S. National Debt by Year," Investopedia, updated May 25, 2025, https://www.investopedia.com/us-national-debt-by-year-7499291.

2   Will Kenton, "What Is the Nixon Shock? Definition, What Happened, and Aftereffects," Investopedia, updated February 8, 2024, https://www.investopedia.com/terms/n/nixon-shock.asp.

3   Srinivasan, "U.S. National Debt by Year."

4   Srinivasan, "U.S. National Debt by Year."

5   Srinivasan, "U.S. National Debt by Year."

6   Srinivasan, "U.S. National Debt by Year."

7   *The Budget and Economic Outlook: 2025 to 2035, by the Numbers* (Congressional Budget Office, 2025), https://www.cbo.gov/system/files/2025-01/60870-By-the-Numbers.pdf.

8   This assumes the population of the United States is 340 million.

9   Robin Saks Frankel, "How Does Your Debt Compare? U.S. Average Credit Card Debt in 2025," *Forbes*, last audited July 3, 2025, https://www.forbes.com/advisor/credit-cards/average-credit-card-debt.

10 Board of Governors of the Federal Reserve System, "Consumer Loans: Credit Cards and Other Revolving Plans, All Commercial Banks," Federal Reserve Bank of St. Louis, last accessed July 8, 2025, https://fred.stlouisfed.org/series/CCLACBM027SBOG.

11 Melanie Hanson, "Student Loan Debt Statistics," Education Data Initiative, last updated March 16, 2025, https://educationdata.org/student-loan-debt-statistics.

12 Maggie Davis, "Average Car Payment and Auto Loan Statistics: 2025," LendingTree, updated June 17, 2025, https://www.lendingtree.com/auto/debt-statistics.

13 Aliss Higham, "2025 Sees Rise in Americans Living Paycheck to Paycheck," *Newsweek*, September 14, 2025, https://www.newsweek.com/2025-rise-americans-living-paycheck-2128753.

14 U.S. Census Bureau and U.S. Department of Housing and Urban Development, "Average Sales Price of Houses Sold for the United States," Federal Reserve Bank of St. Louis, accessed July 8, 2025, https://fred.stlouisfed.org/series/ASPUS.

15   Board of Governors of the Federal Reserve System, "M2 (M2SL)," Federal Reserve Bank of St. Louis, last accessed July 14, 2025, https://fred.stlouisfed.org /series/M2SL.

16   See U.S. Census Bureau and U.S. Department of Housing and Urban Development, "Average Sales Price of Houses Sold for the United States."

17   "Home Price to Median Household Income Ratio," Longtermtrends, accessed September 30, 2025, https://www.longtermtrends.net/home-price-median-annual-income-ratio, citing data from the U.S. Census Bureau and the Federal Reserve Bank of St. Louis.

18   See "Home Price to Median Household Income Ratio."

19   See "Home Price to Median Household Income Ratio."

20   See "S&P 500 – 100 Year Historical Chart," MacroTrends, last accessed July 8, 2025, https://www.macrotrends.net/2324/sp-500-historical-chart-data.

21   See "S&P 500 – 100 Year Historical Chart."

22   "What Are Derivatives?," Fidelity, February 25, 2025, https://www.fidelity.com /learning-center/trading-investing/what-are-derivatives.

23   J. B. Maverick, "How Big Is the Derivatives Market?," Investopedia, updated February 6, 2024, https://www.investopedia.com/ask/answers/052715/how-big -derivatives-market.asp.

24   Jack Kelly, "These Jobs Will Fall First as AI Takes Over the Workplace," Forbes, April 25, 2025, https://www.forbes.com/sites/jackkelly/2025/04/25/the-jobs -that-will-fall-first-as-ai-takes-over-the-workplace.

25   Andrew J. Hawkins, "Aurora's Driverless Trucks Are Making Deliveries in Texas," The Verge, May 1, 2025, https://www.theverge.com/news/659518 /aurora-autonomous-truck-first-delivery-texas.

26   Dario Caldara et al., "The Effect of the War in Ukraine on Global Activity and Inflation," FEDS Notes, Board of Governance of the Federal Reserve System, May 27, 2022, https://www.federalreserve.gov/econres/notes/feds-notes/the -effect-of-the-war-in-ukraine-on-global-activity-and-inflation-20220527.html.

27   Yimou Lee and Ben Blanchard, "Exclusive: China Flexes Military Muscle with East Asian Naval Activity, Sources Say," Reuters, May 28, 2025, https://www .reuters.com/world/china/china-flexes-military-muscle-with-east-asian-naval -activity-sources-say-2025-05-28.

28   Jonathan Masters and Will Merrow, "U.S. Military Support for Taiwan in Five Charts," Council on Foreign Relations, September 25, 2024, https://www.cfr.org /article/us-military-support-taiwan-five-charts.

29   Shobhit Seth, "Why China Buys U.S. Debt with Treasury Bonds," Investopedia, updated February 25, 2025, https://www.investopedia.com/articles /investing/040115/reasons-why-china-buys-us-treasury-bonds.asp.

30   Bailey Schulz and Betty Lin-Fisher, "Will Iran Retaliate? US Officials Warn of

Cyber Attack Risks After Strikes," *USA Today*, June 24, 2025, https://www
.usatoday.com/story/money/2025/06/23/could-iran-launch-cyber-attack
-protect/84322009007.

31   Dana M. Peterson, "U.S. Commercial Real Estate Is Headed Toward a Crisis,"
Harvard Business Review, July 23, 2024, https://hbr.org/2024/07/u-s
-commercial-real-estate-is-headed-toward-a-crisis.

32   Peterson, "U.S. Commercial Real Estate Is Headed Toward a Crisis."

33   "The Depository Trust Company (DTC)," Depository Trust and Clearing
Corporation, accessed August 12, 2025, https://www.dtcc.com/about
/businesses-and-subsidiaries/dtc.

34   "About DTCC," Depository Trust and Clearing Corporation, accessed August
12, 2025, https://www.dtcc.com/about.

35   "DTCC's Businesses, Subsidiaries and Joint Ventures," Depository Trust and
Clearing Corporation, accessed August 12, 2025, https://www.dtcc.com/about
/businesses-and-subsidiaries.

36   "Investor Bulletin: Holding Your Securities," U.S. Securities and Exchange
Commission, July 12, 2023, https://www.investor.gov/introduction-investing
/general-resources/news-alerts/alerts-bulletins/investor-bulletins-97.

37   "Issuer Services," Depository Trust and Clearing Corporation, accessed August
10, 2025, https://www.dtcc.com/issuer-services/index.html.

38   James Chen, "What Is the Depository Trust and Clearing Corporation
(DTCC)?," Investopedia, updated April 12, 2023, https://www.investopedia
.com/terms/d/dtcc.asp.

39   I've chosen to keep this source's name private, because the individual continues
to operate a successful investment business and I want to prevent my source
from being negatively impacted by our conversation and this book.

40   *Investor Bulletin: DTC Chills and Freezes* (SEC Office of Investor Education and
Advocacy, May 2012), https://www.sec.gov/investor/alerts/dtcfreezes.pdf.

41   Will Kenton, "Pro Rata: What It Means and the Formula to Calculate It,"
Investopedia, updated July 4, 2024, https://www.investopedia.com/terms/p/pro
-rata.asp.

42   Another good source that clearly explains how securities ownership works in
regard to DTC is *Demystifying DTC: The Depository Trust Company and the
Municipal Bond Market* (National Association of Bond Lawyers, March 2017): 4,
https://www.nabl.org/wp-content/uploads/2023/02/20170331-NABL
-Demystifying-DTC.pdf.

43   "Uniform Commercial Code," Uniform Law Commission, last accessed May 24,
2024, https://www.uniformlaws.org/acts/ucc.

44   "UCC Article 8, Investment Securities," Uniform Law Commission, accessed
August 12, 2025, https://www.uniformlaws.org/committees/community
-home?CommunityKey=f93a92b2-020f-4bfa-880b-5f80d24d018d.

45 Uniform Commercial Code §8-503(a), Legal Information Institute, Cornell Law School, accessed August 12, 2025, https://www.law.cornell.edu/ucc/8/8-503.

46 Uniform Commercial Code §8-511(b), Legal Information Institute, Cornell Law School, accessed August 12, 2025, https://www.law.cornell.edu/ucc/8/8-511.

47 James S. Rogers, "Policy Perspectives on Revised U.C.C. Article 8," *UCLA Law Review* 43, no. 1431 (1996): 1436, available from Boston College Law School, https://lira.bc.edu/work/sc/81b6ffe2-96c3-4087-b991-c70aaa870a47.

48 Rogers, "Policy Perspectives," 1447.

49 Paul M. Shupack, memorandum to Members of the Uniform State Laws Committee of the Association of the Bar of the City of New York, June 6, 1995, quoted in Francis Jay Facciolo, "Father Knows Best, Revised Article 8 and the Individual Investor," *Florida State University Law Review* 27, no. 3 (2000): 626, https://papers.ssrn.com/sol3/papers.cfm?abstract_id=3357689.

50 Kathleen Patchel, "Interest Group Politics, Federalism, and the Uniform Law Process: Some Lessons from the Uniform Commercial Code," *Minnesota Law Review* 78, no. 83 (1993): 123, https://scholarship.law.umn.edu/mlr/1734/. It should be noted that Patchel's analysis focuses primarily on the Uniform Commercial Code process as a whole and, in this instance, on the drafting of Article 4 rather than on specific revisions to Article 8. However, her detailed account of interest-group influence and procedural dynamics is directly applicable to understanding how the Article 8 amendments were developed.

51 Patchel, "Interest Group Politics, Federalism, and the Uniform Law Process," 144.

52 Patchel, "Interest Group Politics, Federalism, and the Uniform Law Process," 104.

53 Patchel, "Interest Group Politics, Federalism, and the Uniform Law Process," 164.

54 Facciolo, "Father Knows Best," 705.

55 Facciolo, "Father Knows Best," 705.

56 Facciolo, "Father Knows Best," 624.

57 Facciolo, "Father Knows Best," 655.

58 Russell A. Hakes, "UCC Article 8: Will the Indirect Holding of Securities Survive the Light of Day?," *Loyola of Los Angeles Law Review* 35, no. 3 (2002): 689, https://digitalcommons.lmu.edu/llr/vol35/iss3/2/.

59 Hakes, "UCC Article 8," 689.

60 Hakes, "UCC Article 8," 691.

61 Hakes, "UCC Article 8," 784–785.

62 Hakes, "UCC Article 8," 785

63 Hakes, "UCC Article 8," 785.

64   Facciolo, "Father Knows Best," 617.

65   Jack McPherrin, "Revising UCC Article 8 to Put Investors First—Not Wall Street," The Heartland Institute, September 5, 2025, https://heartland.org /publications/revising-ucc-article-8-to-put-investors-first-not-wall-street/.

66   Facciolo, "Father Knows Best," 714. Facciolo excoriates the process by which the changes were made, concluding, "As the states in turn have abdicated their traditional role by not fully examining Revised Article 8, we are left relying on the policy arguments of the supporters. . . . Ultimately, we are hoping that father knows best."

67   "Customer Protection Rule," Legal Information Institute, Cornell Law School, accessed August 10, 2025, https://www.law.cornell.edu/wex/customer _protection_rule.

68   Securities Exchange Act of 1934 § 12(k)(2), 15 U.S.C. § 78l(k)(2), available via Columbia Law School, https://www.columbia.edu/~hcs14/SX12k.htm.

69   U.S. Securities and Exchange Commission, "Emergency Order Pursuant to Section 12(k)(2) of the Securities Exchange Act of 1934 Taking Temporary Action to Respond to Market Developments," Release Number 44791, September 14, 2001, https://www.sec.gov/rules-regulations/2001/09/emergency -order-pursuant-section-12k2-securities-exchange-act-1934-taking-temporary -action-respond.

70   U.S. Securities and Exchange Commission, "Emergency Order Pursuant to Section 12(k)(2) of the Securities Exchange Act of 1934 Taking Temporary Action to Respond to Market Developments," Release Number 58166, July 15, 2008, https://www.sec.gov/files/rules/other/2008/34-58166.pdf.

71   International Emergency Economic Powers Act (IEEPA), 50 U.S.C. §§ 1701– 1710, available via Cornell University Law School, https://www.law.cornell.edu /uscode/text/50/chapter-35.

72   National Emergencies Act (NEA), 50 U.S.C. §§ 1601–1651, available via Cornell University Law School, https://www.law.cornell.edu/uscode/text/50/chapter-34.

73   The U.S. Treasury's Office of Foreign Assets Control administers at least thirty-seven different comprehensive or selective sanctions regimes as of August 10, 2025, in addition to a host of less severe sanctions programs. See "Sanctions Programs and Country Information," Office of Foreign Assets Control, U.S. Department of the Treasury, accessed August 10, 2025, https://ofac.treasury.gov/ sanctions-programs-and-country-information.

74   See The International Emergency Economic Powers Act: Origins, Evolution, and Use (Congressional Research Service, January 30, 2024), https://www.congress .gov/crs-product/R45618. This report states, "While IEEPA nominally applies only to foreign transactions, the breadth of the phrase, 'any interest of any foreign country or a national thereof' leaves a great deal of room for executive discretion. The interconnectedness of the modern global economy has left few major transactions in which a foreign interest is not involved. As a result, at

least one scholar has concluded, 'the exemption of purely domestic transactions from the President's transaction controls seems a limitation without substance.'" The report also states, "The limitation of IEEPA to transactions involving some foreign domestic interest was intended to limit IEEPA's domestic application. However, globalization has eroded that limit, as few transactions today do not involve some foreign interest."

75   Dodd-Frank Wall Street Reform and Consumer Protection Act, Title II, "Orderly Liquidation Authority," 12 U.S.C. §§ 5381–5394, available from Cornell Law School, https://www.law.cornell.edu/uscode/text/12/chapter-53/subchapter-II.

76   U.S. Commodity Futures Trading Commission, "CFTC Orders JPMorgan Chase Bank, N.A. to Pay a $20 Million Civil Monetary Penalty to Settle CFTC Charges of Unlawfully Handling Customer Segregated Funds," news release, no. 6225-12, April 4, 2012, https://www.cftc.gov/PressRoom/PressReleases/6225-12.

77   Commodity Futures Trading Commission, "In the Matter of JPMorgan Chase Bank, N.A.," CFTC Docket No. 12-17, April 4, 2012, https://www.cftc.gov/sites/default/files/idc/groups/public/%40lrenforcementactions/documents/legalpleading/enfjpmorganorder040412.pdf.

78   "The Orderly Liquidation of Lehman Brothers Holdings Inc. Under the Dodd-Frank Act," FDIC Quarterly 5, no. 2 (2011), https://www.fdic.gov/analysis/quarterly-banking-profile/fdic-quarterly/2011-vol5-2/lehman.pdf.

79   Securities Investor Protection Corporation (SIPC), "SIPC Applauds Lehman Trustee on Milestone 100 Percent Return of Securities Customers' Property," news release, June 7, 2013, https://www.sipc.org/news-and-media/news-releases/20130607.

80   U.S. Commodity Futures Trading Commission, Complaint, CFTC v. Sentinel Management Group, Inc., No. 08-CV-2410 (N.D. Ill. April 28, 2008), https://www.cftc.gov/sites/default/files/idc/groups/public/%40lrenforcementactions/documents/legalpleading/enfcomplaintsentinel044808.pdf.

81   U.S. Securities and Exchange Commission, Complaint, SEC v. Sentinel Management Group, Inc., No. 07-4684 (N.D. Ill. Aug. 22, 2007), https://www.sec.gov/files/litigation/complaints/2007/comp20249.pdf.

82   Jonathan Stempel, "Bank of NY Mellon Settles $312 Million Claim Tied to Sentinel Fraud," Reuters, June 30, 2016, https://www.reuters.com/article/world/bank-of-ny-mellon-settles-312-million-claim-tied-to-sentinel-fraud-idUSKCN0ZG3AD/.

83   "In Re: Sentinel Management Group, Inc.," 728 F.3d 660, 666–69 (7th Cir. 2013), https://media.ca7.uscourts.gov/cgi-bin/rssExec.pl?Path=Y2013%2FD08-26%2FC%3A10-3990%3AJ%3ATinder%3Aaut%3AT%3AfnOp%3AN%3A1192594%3AS%3A0&Submit=Display.

84   Frederick J. Grede v. Bank of New York Mellon Corp., 809 F.3d 958, 962–70 (7th Cir. 2016), https://www.mintz.com/sites/default/files/viewpoints

/orig/18/2016/02/In-re-Sentinel-Management-Group-Inc..pdf.

85   U.S. Commodity Futures Trading Commission, "CFTC Charges MF Global Inc.,
     MF Global Holdings Ltd., Former CEO Jon S. Corzine, and Former Employee
     Edith O'Brien for MF Global's Unlawful Misuse of Nearly One Billion Dollars
     of Customer Funds and Related Violations," Press Release, no. 6626-13, June 27,
     2013, https://www.cftc.gov/PressRoom/PressReleases/6626-13.

86   Congressional Research Service, "The MF Global Bankruptcy, Missing
     Customer Funds, and Proposals for Reform," August 1, 2013, https://www
     .congress.gov/crs-product/R42091.

87   U.S. Senate Committee on Agriculture, Nutrition, and Forestry, Investigative
     Hearing of the MF Global Bankruptcy, 112th Congress, First Session, December
     13, 2011, https://www.agriculture.senate.gov/hearings/investigative-hearing-on
     -the-mf-global-bankruptcy.

88   "In re MF Global Inc.," No. 11-2790 (MG) (Bankr. S.D.N.Y., April 26, 2012),
     Order Granting Motion of James W. Giddens, SIPA Trustee for Liquidation of
     MF Global Inc., to Approve First Interim Distribution for Allowed Commodity
     Futures Claims, https://www.cftc.gov/sites/default/files/idc/groups
     /public/%40newsroom/documents/file/authorizingorder042612.pdf.

89   SIPC, "SIPC Commends MF Global Trustee for Achieving Milestone 100
     Percent Return of MF Global Customer Property with Final Distribution," news
     release, April 3, 2014, https://www.sipc.org/news-and-media/news
     -releases/20140403.

90   There are exceptions in certain circumstances. Although difficult to prove, if a
     court determines the secured creditor knew or should have known the assets
     were pledged improperly, their priority claim may be voided. This occurred
     in the Grede v. Bank of New York Mellon litigation following the Sentinel
     Management Group bankruptcy, in which the court ruled the bank should have
     known the assets were being used in violation of segregation requirements. Still,
     as noted earlier, it took nearly nine years for this determination to be made and
     for customers to recover their property.

91   *Disclosure Framework for Covered Clearing Agencies and Financial Market
     Infrastructures* (The Depository Trust Company, March 2023), https://www
     .dtcc.com/-/media/Files/Downloads/legal/policy-and-compliance/DTC
     _Disclosure_Framework.pdf.

92   *Disclosure Framework.*

93   *Disclosure Framework.*

94   "Designated Financial Market Utilities," Board of Governors of the Federal
     Reserve System, last accessed May 24, 2024, https://www.federalreserve.gov
     /paymentsystems/designated_fmu_about.htm.

95   Mark A. Calabria, "If Anyone Needs an Audit, It's the Federal Reserve," Cato
     Institute, February 3, 2015, https://www.cato.org/publications/commentary
     /anyone-needs-audit-its-federal-reserve.

96   Calabria, "If Anyone Needs an Audit."

97   Calabria, "If Anyone Needs an Audit."

98   12 U.S. Code § 95, made available online by Cornell Law School, https://www
.law.cornell.edu/uscode/text/12/95.

99   "What Is SIPC?," SIPC, last accessed May 24, 2024, https://www.sipc.org/for
-investors/introduction.

100   Fidelity, "Safeguarding Your Fidelity Account and Assets," last accessed January
1, 2025, https://www.fidelity.com/misc/ekits/pdf/safeguarding_your_account
.pdf.

101   "The SIPC Fund," SIPC, last accessed July 15, 2025, https://www.sipc.org/about
-sipc/the-sipc-fund.

102   Fidelity, "About Fidelity: By the Numbers," last accessed September 1, 2025,
https://www.fidelity.com/about-fidelity/our-company#.

103   Fidelity, "Safeguarding Your Fidelity Account and Assets."

104   See, for example, Adam Hayes, "Bailment: Definition, How It Works, Types, and
When It Ends," Investopedia, updated June 15, 2024, https://www.investopedia
.com/terms/b/bailment.asp.

105   Somer Anderson, "Stocks Then and Now: The 1950s and 1970s," Investopedia,
updated January 26, 2021, https://www.investopedia.com/articles/stocks/09
/stocks-1950s-1970s.asp.

106   "Volume of Trading on New York Stock Exchange," United States Census
Bureau, last accessed June 4, 2025, https://www2.census.gov/library
/publications/2011/compendia/statab/131ed/tables/12s1210.xls.

107   "Volume of Trading on New York Stock Exchange."

108   "Markets Diary," Wall Street Journal, June 3, 2025, https://www.wsj.com/market
-data/stocks/marketsdiary?gaa_at=eafs&gaa_n=ASWzDAjaRU67-iEOhMUfOH
mOWQJyHDoIlNZLg30ErdG6HszpTsusBO0cqG_ZFIPtOGE%3D&gaa
_ts=68407c56&gaa_sig=Cw7aqMlUqpx_ufQZ8CiysIKMH6i3H6dUfAOx
-vwZGsKYunoI5fs2baMaTB-RqURaCRvbEBEEuLDADgAqjxW5hw%3D%3D.

109   Terry Robards, "Merrill: New Stage," New York Times, May 2, 1971, https://www.
nytimes.com/1971/05/02/archives/merrill-new-stage-merrill
-opens-the-door.html#:~:text=The%20Merrill%20Lynch%20offering%20
should,%E2%80%A2.

110   "Inflation Calculator," Federal Reserve Bank of Minneapolis, accessed August
16, 2025, https://www.minneapolisfed.org/about-us/monetary-policy/inflation
-calculator.

111   Kenneth Corbin, "Merrill Lynch Brings More Wealthy Clients to Its Fee-Based
Advisory Program," Barron's, January 16, 2025, https://www.barrons.com
/advisor/articles/merrill-lynch-wealth-management-earnings-1408fa0e.

112   William Jaenike, interview by James Stocker, SEC Historical Society, July 13,

2011, https://www.sechistorical.org/collection/oral-histories/20110713_Jaenike_William_T.pdf.

113 Jaenike, interview.

114 Maverick, "How Big Is the Derivatives Market?"

115 "Uniform Commercial Code," Uniform Law Commission.

116 The text of the next several paragraphs of this chapter is a condensed and rewritten version of text contained in Justin Haskins, "Why Lawmakers Shouldn't Trust the Uniform Law Commission or American Law Institute," Heartland Institute, June 13, 2024, https://heartland.org/publications/why-lawmakers-shouldnt-trust-the-uniform-law-commission-or-american-law-institute-two-of-americas-biggest-threats-to-freedom/. The text has been published with permission.

117 Though outside the scope of this chapter, leaders and high-ranking members of the Uniform Law Commission and American Law Institute have taken stances on contentious social and cultural topics that raise concerns for many Americans. For a more detailed examination of these positions and other problematic affiliations with individuals and organizations known for championing centralized power, see Haskins, "Why Lawmakers Shouldn't Trust the Uniform Law Commission."

118 "Professor Richard L. Revesz," American Law Institute, last accessed September 15, 2025, https://www.ali.org/profile/4574.

119 "Richard Revesz Confirmed as Head of the White House OMB's Office of Information and Regulatory Affairs," NYU School of Law, December 29, 2022, https://www.law.nyu.edu/news/richard-revesz-oira-confirmation.

120 Jennifer Hijazi, "New Regulation Head Revesz Seen as Most Progressive Rules Czar," Bloomberg Law, December 22, 2022, https://news.bloomberglaw.com/environment-and-energy/new-regulation-head-revesz-seen-as-most-progressive-rules-czar.

121 This is a general description of the position provided by the Obama administration, as shown in "Office of Information and Regulatory Affairs," Office of Management and Budget, last accessed May 14, 2024, https://obamawhitehouse.archives.gov/omb/oira.

122 Hijazi, "Revesz Seen as Most Progressive Rules Czar."

123 "The Hon. Diane P. Wood," American Law Institute, last accessed July 16, 2025, https://www.ali.org/profile/6089.

124 Wood has issued rulings on social and cultural issues not discussed here because they fall outside the scope of this chapter. Some of these decisions are deeply troubling. For further discussion, see Haskins, "Why Lawmakers Shouldn't Trust the Uniform Law Commission."

125 "The Hon. Diane P. Wood."

126 Bevis v. City of Naperville (7th Cir. 2023), https://tinyurl.com/32hvk2w3.

127 Illinois Republican Party v. Pritzker (7th Cir. 2020), https://tinyurl.com
     /ys2zwjmj.

128 "Janet Napolitano Appointed to President's Intelligence Advisory Board,"
     American Law Institute, May 12, 2022, https://www.ali.org/news/articles/janet
     -napolitano-appointed-presidents-intelligence-advisory-board.

129 "Professor Janet Napolitano," American Law Institute, accessed August 8, 2025,
     https://www.ali.org/profile/3694.

130 "The American Law Institute Council," American Law Institute, accessed
     August 8, 2025, https://www.ali.org/council-members.

131 "Public-Health Emergency Authority Act," Uniform Law Commission, last
     accessed January 6, 2025, https://www.uniformlaws.org/committees
     /community-home?CommunityKey=7a88c160-5910-4e41-9dff-018a850ef3b2.

132 For a more in-depth legal analysis of the PHEAA, see Don Grande, "The Public-
     Health Emergency Authority Act: A Framework for Unchecked Gubernatorial
     Power," Heartland Institute, December 15, 2023, https://heartland.org
     /publications/the-public-health-emergency-authorization-act-a-framework-for
     -unchecked-gubernatorial-power/.

133 "Public-Health Emergency Authority Act."

134 "Public-Health Emergency Authority Act."

135 See "UCC, 2022 Amendments to," Uniform Law Commission, accessed August
     8, 2025, https://www.uniformlaws.org/committees/community
     -home?CommunityKey=1457c422-ddb7-40b0-8c76-39a1991651ac.

136 For more information about the 2022 UCC amendments, how they facilitate a
     CBDC, and how they lay the groundwork for centralized control of real-world
     assets through tokenization, see Jack McPherrin and Daylea DuVall Camp, "The
     2022 Amendments to the Uniform Commercial Code Abrogate Property Rights
     to Tangible Assets," Heartland Institute, September 18, 2024, https://heartland
     .org/publications/the-2022-amendments-to-the-uniform-commercial-code
     -abrogate-property-rights-to-tangible-assets/.

137 "UCC, 2022 Amendments to."

138 Facciolo, "Father Knows Best."

139 For more information about the amendments to the Uniform Commercial Code
     introduced in the 1970s, see James S. Rogers, "Policy Perspectives on Revised
     U.C.C. Article 8," UCLA Law Review 43, no. 1431 (1996), https://lira.bc.edu
     /work/sc/81b6ffe2-96c3-4087-b991-c70aaa870a47.

140 William Dentzer, interview by James Stocker, SEC Historical Society, July
     20, 2011, https://www.sechistorical.org/collection/oral-histories/20110720_
     Dentzer_William_T.pdf.

141 Dentzer, interview.

142 Dentzer, interview.

143 See the previous chapter for more information about the Depository Trust Company, how the modern securities market works, and the potential economic risks posed by the immobilization of securities.

144 James R. Hagerty, "William Dentzer Helped Wall Street Unsnarl Its Paperwork," *Wall Street Journal*, updated February 11, 2021, https://www.wsj.com/articles /william-dentzer-helped-wall-street-unsnarl-its-paperwork-11613055610.

145 Susan Dentzer and William Dentzer, "The Greatest Father from a Great Generation," Medium, August 27, 2019, https://susan-g-dentzer.medium.com /the-greatest-father-from-a-great-generation-f9ceb3758066.

146 Dentzer and Dentzer, "Greatest Father from a Great Generation."

147 See the previous chapter of this book for more.

148 *A Short History of the Depository Trust Company* (SEC Historical Society, 1999), https://www.sechistorical.org/collection/papers/1990/1999_0101 _DTCHistory.pdf.

149 *A Short History of the Depository Trust Company*.

150 *A Short History of the Depository Trust Company*.

151 *A Short History of the Depository Trust Company*.

152 *A Short History of the Depository Trust Company*.

153 *A Short History of the Depository Trust Company*.

154 *A Short History of the Depository Trust Company*.

155 *A Short History of the Depository Trust Company*.

156 Dentzer, interview.

157 Dentzer, interview.

158 Hagerty, "Dentzer Helped Wall Street."

159 Dentzer, interview.

160 Dentzer, interview.

161 Dentzer, interview.

162 Dentzer and Dentzer, "Greatest Father from a Great Generation."

163 Based on the extensive research I've conducted, it appears Dentzer never lived or worked in New York before his arrival in 1969. However, it's possible he had a position I'm not aware of.

164 Some might say working as the top New York bank regulator qualifies as "working on Wall Street," but I don't think most would take this view, and I certainly do not. Therefore, I think my assertion here is accurate.

165 Dentzer, interview.

166 Dentzer and Dentzer, "Greatest Father from a Great Generation."

167 Dentzer and Dentzer, "Greatest Father from a Great Generation."

168 Dentzer and Dentzer, "Greatest Father from a Great Generation."

169 Dentzer and Dentzer, "Greatest Father from a Great Generation."

170 Dentzer and Dentzer, "Greatest Father from a Great Generation."

171 Neil Sheehan, "A Student Group Concedes It Took Funds from C.I.A.," *New York Times*, February 14, 1967, https://www.nytimes.com/1967/02/14/archives/a -student-group-concedes-it-took-funds-from-cia-national.html.

172 Dentzer and Dentzer, "Greatest Father from a Great Generation."

173 Karen Paget, *Patriotic Betrayal* (Yale University Press, 2015).

174 Dentzer and Dentzer, "Greatest Father from a Great Generation."

175 Paget, *Patriotic Betrayal*.

176 Dentzer and Dentzer, "Greatest Father from a Great Generation."

177 Dentzer, interview.

178 Paget, *Patriotic Betrayal*.

179 "Karen M. Paget," karenmpaget.com, last accessed April 24, 2025, https:// karenmpaget.com/bio.

180 Paget, *Patriotic Betrayal*.

181 Paget, *Patriotic Betrayal*.

182 Paget, *Patriotic Betrayal*.

183 Dentzer and Dentzer, "Greatest Father from a Great Generation."

184 Paget, *Patriotic Betrayal*.

185 Paget, *Patriotic Betrayal*.

186 Paget, *Patriotic Betrayal*.

187 Stuart H. Loory, "How Deep Its Ties? Hotel Room Death Showed Student Link," *Miami Herald* and *Los Angeles Times*, February 26, 2025.

188 Loory, "How Deep Its Ties?"

189 Loory, "How Deep Its Ties?"

190 Loory, "How Deep Its Ties?"

191 Loory, "How Deep Its Ties?"

192 Dentzer and Dentzer, "Greatest Father from a Great Generation."

193 Dentzer and Dentzer, "Greatest Father from a Great Generation."

194 Dentzer, interview.

195 Dentzer, interview.

196 Peter Kornbluh, "Secret Programs Hurt Foreign Aid Efforts," *New York Times*, December 16, 2014, https://www.nytimes.com/roomfordebate/2014/04/15 /when-is-foreign-aid-meddling/secret-programs-hurt-foreign-aid-efforts.

197 Catherine A. Traywick, "'Cuban Twitter' and Other Times USAID Pretended to Be an Intelligence Agency," Foreign Policy, April 3, 2014, https://foreignpolicy.com/2014/04/03/cuban-twitter-and-other-times-usaid-pretended-to-be-an-intelligence-agency.

198 Department of State, "Document 253," in Foreign Relations of the United States: 1964–1968, ed. Edward C. Keefer et al., vol. XXXI, South and Central America; Mexico (United States Government Printing Office, 2004), https://history.state.gov/historicaldocuments/frus1964-68v31/d253.

199 "Document 253" in Foreign Relations of the United States.

200 Dentzer, interview.

201 Department of State, "Persons," in Foreign Relations of the United States: 1964–1968, ed. Edward C. Keefer et al., vol. XXXI, South and Central America; Mexico (United States Government Printing Office, 2004), https://history.state.gov/historicaldocuments/frus1964-68v31/persons.

202 See footnote 1 in "Document 253" in Foreign Relations of the United States.

203 James Doubek, "The U.S. Set the Stage for a Coup in Chile: It Had Unintended Consequences at Home," NPR, September 10, 2023, https://www.npr.org/2023/09/10/1193755188/chile-coup-50-years-pinochet-kissinger-human-rights-allende.

204 Peruvian Seizure of IPC Assets (CIA, January 1, 1969), https://www.cia.gov/readingroom/document/cia-rdp78-03061a000400020009-8.

205 Peruvian Seizure of IPC Assets.

206 See "Document 511," in Foreign Relations of the United States: 1964–1968, ed. Edward C. Keefer et al., vol. XXXI, South and Central America; Mexico (United States Government Printing Office, 2004), https://history.state.gov/historicaldocuments/frus1964-68v31/d511.

207 Peruvian Seizure of IPC Assets.

208 Peruvian Seizure of IPC Assets.

209 Peruvian Seizure of IPC Assets.

210 The IPC Case: As Controversial as Ever (CIA, July 21, 1972), https://www.cia.gov/readingroom/docs/CIA-RDP85T00875R002000120005-8.pdf.

211 The IPC Case: As Controversial as Ever.

212 The IPC Case: As Controversial as Ever.

213 "Document 478" in Foreign Relations of the United States: 1964–1968, ed. Edward C. Keefer et al., vol. XXXI, South and Central America; Mexico (United States Government Printing Office, 2004), https://history.state.gov/historicaldocuments/frus1964-68v31/d478.

214 See "Oil: Including the Special Cases of Peru and Venezuela," North American Congress on Latin America, September 25, 2007, citing an article published by

TIME magazine on December 29, 1967, https://nacla.org/article/oil-including-special-cases-peru-and-venezuela?utm_source=chatgpt.com.

215 Dentzer, interview.

216 Dentzer and Dentzer, "Greatest Father from a Great Generation."

217 Dentzer, interview.

218 Dentzer, interview.

219 Paget, *Patriotic Betrayal*.

220 Paget, *Patriotic Betrayal*.

221 Dentzer and Dentzer, "Greatest Father from a Great Generation."

222 Paget, *Patriotic Betrayal*.

223 *A Short History of the Depository Trust Company*.

224 Dentzer and Dentzer, "Greatest Father from a Great Generation."

225 Jaenike, interview.

226 Jaenike, interview.

227 Sam Roberts, "Robert Kiley, Mass Transit Chief in Boston, London and New York, Dies at 80," *New York Times*, August 9, 2016, https://www.nytimes.com/2016/08/10/nyregion/robert-kiley-mass-transit-dead.html.

228 Paget, *Patriotic Betrayal*.

229 Paget, *Patriotic Betrayal*.

230 Paget, *Patriotic Betrayal*.

231 Graeme Zielinski, "Key CIA Figure Cord Meyer Dies," *Washington Post*, March 14, 2001, https://www.washingtonpost.com/archive/local/2001/03/15/key-cia-figure-cord-meyer-dies/fc90ef11-4137-4582-9f01-c7c13461e1bf.

232 Leena Kim, "Inside the Unsolved Murder of JFK's Mistress Mary Pinchot Meyer," *Town & Country*, May 25, 2020, https://www.townandcountrymag.com/leisure/arts-and-culture/a32599090/mary-meyer-jfk-mistress-murder.

233 "Woman Painter Shot and Killed on Canal Towpath in Capital; Mrs. Mary Pinchot Meyer Was a Friend of Mrs. Kennedy—Suspect Is Arraigned," *New York Times*, October 14, 1964, https://www.nytimes.com/1964/10/14/archives/woman-painter-shot-and-killed-on-canal-towpath-in-capital-mrs-mary.html.

234 "Central Bank Digital Currency (CBDC)," Board of Governors of the Federal Reserve System, last updated April 11, 2023, https://www.federalreserve.gov/cbdc-faqs.htm.

235 "Central Bank Digital Currency (CBDC)."

236 Bo Erickson, "Biden Issues Executive Order to Explore Cryptocurrency-Like Digital Dollar," *CBS News*, updated March 9, 2022, https://www.cbsnews.com/news/cryptocurrency-biden-executive-order-digital-dollar/?utm

_source=chatgpt.com.

237 Roger Huang, "A 2025 Overview of the E-CNY, China's Digital Yuan," *Forbes*, July 15, 2024, https://www.forbes.com/sites/digital-assets/2024/07/15/a-2024 -overview-of-the-e-cny-chinas-digital-yuan.

238 "Historical Background and Development of Social Security," Social Security Administration, last accessed June 7, 2025, https://www.ssa.gov/history /briefhistory3.html.

239 "Japanese-American Incarceration During World War II," National Archives, last reviewed March 24, 2024, https://www.archives.gov/education/lessons /japanese-relocation#background.

240 "Japanese-American Incarceration."

241 Elizabeth Goitein, "Rolling Back the Post-9/11 Surveillance State," Brennan Center for Justice, August 25, 2021, https://www.brennancenter.org/our-work /analysis-opinion/rolling-back-post-911-surveillance-state.

242 James Chen, "Bretton Woods Agreement and the Institutions It Created," Investopedia, updated April 19, 2025, https://www.investopedia.com/terms/b /brettonwoodsagreement.asp.

243 Jack Rosenthal, "A Terrible Thing to Waste," *New York Times*, July 31, 2009, https://www.nytimes.com/2009/08/02/magazine/02FOB-onlanguage-t.html.

244 Thai-Binh Elston, "China Is Doubling Down on Its Digital Currency," Foreign Policy Research Institute, June 2, 2023, https://www.fpri.org/article/2023/06 /china-is-doubling-down-on-its-digital-currency.

245 Jake Laband, "Existential Threat or Digital Yawn: Evaluating China's Central Bank Digital Currency," *Harvard International Law Journal* 63, no. 2 (2022): 515–559, https://journals.law.harvard.edu/ilj/wp-content/uploads/sites/84 /HLI201_crop-4.pdf.

246 Rita Liao, "China's Digital Yuan Tests Leap Forward in Shenzhen," *TechCrunch*, October 11, 2020, https://techcrunch.com/2020/10/11/china-digital-yuan -shenzhen/.

247 "China Launches Another Public Test of Digital Currency in Suzhou, Supporting Online and Offline Payment," *Global Times*, December 6, 2020, https://www.globaltimes.cn/page/202012/1209124.shtml.

248 Gu Ting and Chen Zifei, "China Pilots Paying Civil Servant Salaries in Digital Yuan Cryptocurrency," Radio Free Asia, May 25, 2023, https://www.rfa.org /english/news/china/china-digital-yuan-05252023221111.html.

249 Huang, "A 2025 Overview of the E-CNY."

250 Carol Yang, "China's Complex Social Credit System Evolves with 23 New Guidelines from Beijing," *South China Morning Post*, April 1, 2025, https://www .scmp.com/economy/article/3304748/chinas-complex-social-credit-system -evolves-23-new-guidelines-beijing.

251 "Assessing China's 'National Model' Social Credit System," Stanford Center on China's Economy and Institutions, July 15, 2025, https://scceichinabriefs .substack.com/p/assessing-chinas-national-model-social.

252 Chuncheng Liu and Akos Rona-Tas, "Trusting by Numbers: An Analysis of a Chinese Social Credit System Governance Infrastructure," *Critical Sociology*, April 15, 2024, https://journals.sagepub.com/doi/10.1177/08969205241246528.

253 John Feng, "How China's Social Credit System Works," *Newsweek*, December 22, 2022, https://www.newsweek.com/china-social-credit-system-works -explained-1768726.

254 Feng, "How China's Social Credit System Works."

255 Feng, "How China's Social Credit System Works."

256 Feng, "How China's Social Credit System Works."

257 James A. Dorn, "China's Digital Yuan: A Threat to Freedom," Cato Institute, August 25, 2021, https://www.cato.org/blog/chinas-digital-yuan-threat-freedom.

258 Sandra Waliczek, "What Are Central Bank Digital Currencies and What Could They Mean for the Average Person?," World Economic Forum, October 6, 2023, https://www.weforum.org/stories/2023/10/what-are-central-bank-digital -currencies-advantages-risks.

259 For example, see Sophia Lopez, "4 Ways to Ensure Central Bank Digital Currencies Promote Financial Inclusion," World Economic Forum, October 13, 2022, https://www.weforum.org/stories/2022/10/4-ways-to-ensure-central -bank-digital-currencies-promote-financial-inclusion.

260 Sandra Waliczek, "Privacy Concerns Around CBDCs—Are They Justified?," World Economic Forum, November 7, 2023, https://www.weforum.org /stories/2023/11/privacy-concerns-around-cbdcs.

261 Chen, "Bretton Woods Agreement."

262 "What Is the IMF?," International Monetary Fund, last accessed August 12, 2025, https://www.imf.org/en/About/Factsheets/IMF-at-a-Glance.

263 Ahmed Eljechtimi, "IMF Working on Global Central Bank Digital Currency Platform," Reuters, June 19, 2023, https://www.reuters.com/markets/imf -working-global-central-bank-digital-currency-platform-2023-06-19.

264 Ceri Parker, "End Fossil Fuel Subsidies and Reset the Economy for a Better World—IMF Head," World Economic Forum, June 3, 2020, https://www .weforum.org/stories/2020/06/end-fossil-fuel-subsidies-economy-imf -georgieva-great-reset-climate.

265 See "Meet Our Experts," Atlantic Council, last accessed June 16, 2025, https:// www.atlanticcouncil.org/people, and "Board of Directors," Atlantic Council, last accessed June 16, 2025, https://www.atlanticcouncil.org/about/board-of -directors.

266 For example, see "Exploring Central Bank Digital Currency: Evaluating

Challenges & Developing International Standards," Atlantic Council, November 28, 2023, https://www.atlanticcouncil.org/event/exploring-central-bank-digital -currency.

267 "Central Bank Digital Currency Tracker," Atlantic Council, last checked June 16, 2025, https://www.atlanticcouncil.org/cbdctracker.

268 "Central Bank Digital Currency Tracker."

269 "Central Bank Digital Currency Tracker."

270 "Fact Sheet: Executive Order to Establish United States Leadership in Digital Financial Technology," White House, January 23, 2025, https://www.whitehouse .gov/fact-sheets/2025/01/fact-sheet-executive-order-to-establish-united-states -leadership-in-digital-financial-technology.

271 Jay Lindsay, "Boston Fed, MIT Complete Research Project into Feasibility of a Central Bank Digital Currency," Federal Reserve Bank of Boston, December 22, 2022, https://www.bostonfed.org/news-and-events/news/2022/12/project -hamilton-boston-fed-mit-complete-central-bank-digital-currency-cbdc -project.aspx.

272 "Project Cedar: Improving Cross-Border Payments with Distributed Ledger Technology," Federal Reserve Bank of New York, last accessed June 16, 2025, https://www.newyorkfed.org/aboutthefed/nyic/project-cedar.

273 "Project Cedar: Improving Cross-Border Payments."

274 Erickson, "Biden Issues Executive Order."

275 *Policy Objectives for a U.S. Central Bank Digital Currency System* (Biden-Harris Administration, 2022), https://bidenwhitehouse.archives.gov/wp -content/uploads/2022/09/09-2022-Policy-Objectives-US-CBDC-System.pdf.

276 Justin Haskins, "Biden's Proposal for a New Digital Currency Is an Attack on Liberty," *Fox Business*, March 26, 2022, https://www.foxbusiness.com/politics /biden-digital-currency-cryptocurrency-justin-haskins.

277 See David Andolfatto, quoted in Laura Taylor, "Navigating the ABCs of CBDCs—Central Bank Digital Currencies," Federal Reserve Bank of St. Louis, June 30, 2021, https://www.stlouisfed.org/open-vault/2021/june/navigating-the -abcs-of-central-bank-digital-currencies.

278 Andolfatto, quoted in Taylor, "Navigating the ABCs of CBDCs."

279 Jeff Cox, "Powell Squashes the Possibility That the Fed Will Develop Its Own Digital Currency," CNBC, updated February 11, 2025, https://www.cnbc. com/2025/02/11/powell-squashes-the-possibility-that-the-fed-will-develop-its -own-digital-currency.html.

280 Kathryn Watson, "Trump Signs Landmark GENIUS Act, Hailing 'Exciting New Frontier' for Crypto," *CBS News*, updated July 18, 2025, https://www.cbsnews .com/news/trump-signs-genius-act-crypto-bill.

281 James Van Straten, "Stablecoin Market Cap Tops $200B as U.S. Sees Industry

Helping Maintain Dollar Dominance," *CoinDesk*, March 10, 2025, https://www
.coindesk.com/markets/2025/03/10/stablecoin-market-cap-tops-usd200b-as-u
-s-sees-industry-helping-maintain-dollar-dominance.

282 Dilip Kumar Patairya, "What Is the GENIUS Act? How It Could Reshape
US Stablecoin Regulation," *Coin Telegraph*, updated April 2, 2025, https://
cointelegraph.com/learn/articles/genius-act-how-it-could-reshape-us
-stablecoin-regulation.

283 Krisztian Sandor, "Stablecoins Could Bring 'ChatGPT' Moment to Blockchain
Adoption, Hit $3.7T by 2030: Citi," *CoinDesk*, April 25, 2025, https://www.
coindesk.com/markets/2025/04/25/stablecoins-could-bring-chatgpt-moment
-for-blockchain-adoption-hit-usd3-7t-by-2030-citi.

284 Jacquelyn Melinek, "BlackRock, Fidelity and Others to Invest $400M in USDC
Stablecoin Issuer Circle," April 12, 2022, *TechCrunch*, https://techcrunch
.com/2022/04/12/blackrock-fidelity-and-others-to-invest-400m-in-usdc
-stablecoin-issuer-circle.

285 For a comprehensive study of BlackRock, see Glenn Beck and Justin Haskins,
Dark Future: Uncovering the Great Reset's Terrifying Next Phase (Forefront
Books, 2023).

286 Andrew Powell, "DeSantis Signs Bill Banning Use of Central Bank Currencies,"
The Center Square, May 12, 2023, https://www.thecentersquare.com/florida
/article_b9834cb8-f0ec-11ed-b73d-0392081ed139.html.

287 Arijit Sarkar, "America Must Back Pro-Stablecoin Laws, Reject CBDCs—US
Rep. Emmer," *Coin Telegraph*, March 12, 2025, https://cointelegraph.com/news
/tom-emmer-pro-stablecoin-bill-cbdcs-un-american.

288 South Dakota State News, "Gov. Noem Signs Bills Blocking Central Bank Digital
Currency," February 27, 2024, https://news.sd.gov/news?id=news_kb_article
_view&sysparm_article=KB0041811&sys_kb
_id=2a60e5b6876042504ec6a75e3fbb355a&spa=1.

289 "11 States Have Pending Anti-CBDC Legislation: South Dakota Votes in Favor,"
Ledger Insights, February 2, 2024, https://www.ledgerinsights.com/11-states
-have-pending-anti-cbdc-legislation-south-dakota-votes-in-favor.

290 Hugh Son, "JPMorgan Chase Says It Will Close 20% of Its Branches Because of
the Coronavirus Pandemic," CNBC, March 18, 2020, https://www.cnbc
.com/2020/03/18/jpmorgan-says-it-will-close-20percent-branches-because
-coronavirus-pandemic.html.

291 Michael Sainato, "'My Savings Were Gone': Millions Who Lost Work During
Covid Faced Benefit System Chaos," *Guardian*, July 22, 2021, https://www
.theguardian.com/us-news/2021/jul/22/unemployment-systems-reform
-pandemic.

292 Jack McPherrin and Justin Haskins, *Policy Tip Sheet: Revising Article 8 of the
Uniform Commercial Code to Protect Americans' Property Rights* (Heartland
Institute, Pro-Family Legislative Network, and Henry Dearborn Liberty

Network, March 12, 2024), https://heartland.org/publications/revising-article-8 -of-the-uniform-commercial-code-to-protect-americans-property-rights.

293 I explained how this might occur in chapter 2.

294 "Tokenized Securities," Coinmarketcap.com, last accessed September 19, 2025, https://coinmarketcap.com/academy/glossary/tokenized-securities.

295 See the Pro-Family Legislative Network (https://profamily.com).

296 See Constitutional Currency (https://transactionalgold.com).

297 For a great book on transaction gold, see Kevin Freeman, *Pirate Money: Discovering the Founders' Hidden Plan for Economic Justice and Defeating the Great Reset* (LibertyHawk Publishing, 2024).

298 Nicole Williams-Quezada and Adam Schwager, "Gold, Silver Become Legal Tender in Texas Under New Law," *KXAN*, July 6, 2025, https://www.kxan.com /news/texas-politics/gold-silver-become-legal-tender-in-texas-under-new-law.

299 NBC6, "DeSantis Signs Bill Recognizing Gold, Silver Coins as Legal Tender in Florida," *NBC Miami*, May 28, 2025, https://www.nbcmiami.com/news /local/desantis-signs-bill-recognizing-gold-silver-coins-as-legal-tender-in -florida/3623981.

300 "Constitutional Amendment Process," National Archives, last accessed July 12, 2025, https://www.archives.gov/federal-register/constitution.

301 "Constitutional Amendment Process."

302 "Constitutional Amendment Process."

303 "Balanced Budget Now," last accessed August 18, 2025, https:// balancedbudgetnow.com.

304 "Progress Map: States That Have Passed the Convention of States Article V Application," Convention of States Action, last accessed July 12, 2025, https:// conventionofstates.com/states-that-have-passed-the-convention-of-states -article-v-application.

ABOUT THE AUTHOR

Justin Haskins is a vice president at The Heartland Institute, a national free-market think tank, and a senior fellow at Our Republic. He's also a *New York Times* bestselling author and a widely published political commentator. Additionally, Haskins serves as the editor in chief of StoppingSocialism.com, one of the world's largest and most influential publications devoted to challenging socialism, and he's the cofounder of Heartland's Emerging Issues Center.

Haskins is a prolific writer who has authored more than one thousand articles in major digital and print publications. He writes most frequently for FoxNews.com, *TheBlaze, The Hill, The Federalist,* and *Townhall.* His work has also been published by *The Wall Street Journal, New York Post, Forbes, Newsweek, National Review,* and many other prominent publications.

Haskins has appeared on television and radio more than four hundred times, including on highly influential shows such as *Tucker Carlson Tonight, Fox & Friends,* and the *Glenn Beck Program.* His analyses and research have been featured by *The Glenn Beck Program, Hannity, Jesse Watters Primetime, Fox & Friends, The New York Times, The Washington Post,* The Heritage Foundation, BlazeTV, *Newsmax,* the White House, and by countless members of Congress and Donald Trump.

Haskins is the author of the Amazon bestselling book *Socialism Is Evil: The Moral Case Against Marx's Radical Dream* (2018), and he is the first contributor to Glenn Beck's *Arguing with Socialists* (2020), a *New York Times* bestselling book.

Haskins is the coauthor, with Beck, of *The Great Reset: Joe Biden and the Rise of 21st Century Fascism* (2022), which appeared on numerous bestselling book lists, including those of *The New York Times, USA Today*, and *The Wall Street Journal*. He also coauthored, with Beck, *Dark Future: Uncovering the Great Reset's Terrifying Next Phase* (2023) and *Propaganda Wars: How the Global Elite Control What You See, Think, and Feel* (2024). *Dark Future* appeared on *The New York Times, The Wall Street Journal*, and *USA Today* bestseller lists.

Haskins graduated with a bachelor's degree from the University of Richmond (Richmond, VA) in 2010. In 2011, Justin earned his master's degree in government with specializations in international relations and American government from Regent University (Virginia Beach, VA). In 2015, he earned a second master's degree, this time in journalism, from Regent University.

Haskins was inducted into The Philadelphia Society in 2018, and he is currently a member of the National Association of Scholars, The Federalist Society, and the National Rifle Association. In 2017, Haskins was named one of *Newsmax's* "Top 30 Republicans under 30."

Most important of all, Haskins is a passionate Christian who imperfectly seeks to live out his faith in all of his work.